"Larry Hayes not only had views, ...issions. By doggedly pursuing them, he changed lives and made extraordinary contributions to Indiana. . . . Larry's own story and the others he tells are an inspiration for all seeking to find their place and work in life." **U.S. Sen. Dick Lugar**

"This book is a fascinating account of his personal efforts coupled with his judicious use of the editorial page to bring about reform that in many cases would not have happened without his involvement. The issues span an impressive spectrum that includes school desegregation, smoking in restaurants, justice for the mentally ill, the treatment of juveniles in the criminal justice system, and others. The book offers hope that change can happen for the better even against heavy opposition." **Ian Rolland, Retired CEO of Lincoln National Corporation**

"What a delight! This memoir is part autobiography, part history, part advocacy, but 100% fascinating. In a time of public cynicism, it feels so good and hopeful to see the courage and determination of ordinary local people lifted up and remembered. . . . Larry not only wrote fearlessly (while maintaining relationships with everyone on all sides), but he drew people together for common cause. During Larry Hayes' many years as a writer at The Journal Gazette, he played a role in nearly every important advancement in public policy in Fort Wayne. Larry was a catalyst, or what the Bible would call leaven. I urge you to read this book!" **The Rev. Dr. Richard Hamm, Former General Minister and President of the Christian Church (Disciples of Christ)**

"Hayes recounts his journey from his childhood in a small Ohio town to aspiring preacher in a conservative seminary to a career as one of Indiana's most influential journalist/advocates. He seemed destined for a pulpit, but his turned out to be in a newsroom rather than a sanctuary. . . . The list of causes Hayes has championed is nearly unprecedented: promoting school desegregation, ending corporal punishment, advocating for the rights of children in the juvenile justice system, fighting against the death penalty, . . . and, perhaps most passionately, raising awareness of society's stigmatization and oppression of persons with mental illness." **William H. Barton, Professor, Indiana University School of Social Work**

"Larry Hayes has a talent for targeting the support and skills of key citizens to help solve social problems and is fearless in the face of obstacles. This book is a compelling and sometimes controversial account of how one person can act as a catalyst for significant community change." **Kathleen O'Connell, Associate Dean, School of Health Sciences, Indiana University-Purdue University Fort Wayne**

"Larry Hayes is an unrepentant activist. The account of his crusades at The Fort Wayne Journal Gazette is a portrait of the editorial writer as social activist. . . . Hayes' book is a rich account of the rewards of editorial activism: elementary schools desegregated, a female juvenile moved out of an adult prison, more humane policies on the treatment of children in schools and the mentally ill in the community. . . . The value of his story is not only in the hope for social changes Hayes wants to engender, but in the debate it can inspire over the editorial writer's role in the community." **David Boeyink, Professor of Journalism at Indiana University**

"In an era of journalists striking a cool, cynical pose, Hayes brought passion to his profession and in the process, transformed a part of the nation. . . . Hayes' way of making a difference was unconventional. . ., but his readers and his community were well served by his willingness to break the mold." **Phil Haslanger, Managing Editor, The Capital Times and Former President of the National Conference of Editorial Writers**

"This is an extraordinary book. Larry Hayes' compassion for the human condition, justice, and fairness shine through in every story of the crusades he launched for what's right from his position as a newspaper editorial writer and columnist. It's inspiring reading for anyone who cares about the plight of human beings." **James C. Howell, Former Head of Research at the U.S. Department of Juvenile Justice and Delinquency Prevention**

"Larry Hayes was an editorial writer with the commitment to justice of an Old Testament prophet and a fierce instinct to protect the powerless. His years at The Journal Gazette and his social activism changed the quality of life for vast numbers of people. Larry has retired from the editorial page, but he continues to be a dedicated worker for positive change. In *Monday I'll Save the World*, he gives both inspiration and practical guidance to people who want to change the system, to create a better world. He shows how ordinary people can make a difference." **Steve Clapp, author of thirty books on congregational life**

Monday I'll Save the World

Memoir of a Heartland Journalist

Larry Hayes

Cover by Custom Maid Design

A LifeQuest Publication

Monday I'll Save the World
Memoir of a Heartland Journalist

Larry Hayes

For further information, contact: LifeQuest, 6404 S. Calhoun Street, Fort Wayne, Indiana 46807; DadofTia@aol.com; 260-456-5010.

Our thanks to Randy Maid for another outstanding cover design and to the staff of Evangel Press for their high standards in manufacturing.

ISBN 1-893270-25-4

Library of Congress Control Number: 2004096558

Manufactured in the United States of America

For Tanya and Cynthia

Acknowledgments

I start with the profound thanks I owe my publishers at The Journal Gazette, Dick Inskeep for most of my tenure and his daughter, Julie Inskeep in the latter years. I tip my hat as well to my editors, Larry Allen who hired and coached me in the arcane art of writing editorials and, beginning in 1982, Craig Klugman, who pushed me to take up crusades and argue the paper's views with passion.

Beyond these folk, I've been blessed with associates, editorial writers and copy editors, journalists whose gifts were only matched by their good hearts. I think of editorial writers George Neavoll, Tim Harmon, Dave Beery, Barbara Morrow, Elma Sabo, Caroline Brewer and Bonnie Blackburn and my deputy Evan Davis. They made journalism fun and enriched my life in the bargain.

My colleagues at LifeQuest have taken up where those at the paper left off. I'm particularly grateful to Steve Clapp. He is my publisher and has become a good friend. His faith in this venture far transcended my imagination. His wise and gentle counsel has saved me from my worst impulses. My editor, Holly Sprunger, has been my too kind critic. I also mention LifeQuest's associates, Stacy Sellers and Kristen Leverton Helbert, whose various tasks helped bring this project to the public.

A special thanks goes to The Journal Gazette's longtime political cartoonist, Dan Lynch. He regularly brought humor with his truths to the pages that tend to take themselves too seriously. In that spirit, at my retirement, he drew the caricature of yours truly that appears on the cover.

There's a group whose forgiveness I now beg - my wife Toni, son John and daughter Robyn, whom I've sometimes embarrassed by mentioning them in columns and who make brief appearances in this memoir. Their forbearance truly has been unearned on my part. With my retirement from the paper, they no doubt hoped to have their anonymity back. Alas, they remain part and parcel of my story.

John graciously and with considerable courage let me write about his battle with mental illness. And I've been blessed beyond measure with my wife Toni. I couldn't have completed one chapter of this book without her patience and encouragement. As my chief proofreader and cheerleader rolled into one, she has no peer.

Of course, no advance in the cause of peace and justice depends on two or three people alone. Rather, it is measured by the sum total of the commitment of each one fighting for the cause. So it is that the victories I recount in this book belong to scores of kindred spirits.

Contents

Foreword by
U.S. Senator Dick Lugar

Larry Hayes was a special editorial writer and editorial page editor to say the least. I was confident each meeting would be filled with respect, with his listening to me, and me listening to his current concerns and causes. Larry did not only have views, he had missions. By doggedly pursuing them, he changed lives and made extraordinary contributions to Indiana.

When he informed me he was writing a book he hoped would encourage others to step out and make a difference I was delighted. *Monday I'll Save the World* caused me to reflect on my own route to the community activism that he advocates so strongly and has inspired me to share here.

Like Larry, I see changes that ought to be made in human affairs and am eager to make things happen. We are excited by the prospect of working with people to bring good ideas to the forefront and to try to achieve the adoption of the better alternatives in the rough and tumble of local, state, or national politics. We enjoy research and discovery and the exhilaration of debate with those who are knowledgeable and committed.

However, that is not how I saw things in May of 1960. I left active duty in the U.S. Navy and returned to Indianapolis to work with my brother Tom to reverse the fortunes of our family's manufacturing and farming businesses because of the untimely death of our father. I had no prospect or idea that I would be elected to anything, let alone the U.S. Senate. Nor had I any inkling that someday I'd chair the Foreign Relations Committee, the Agriculture Committee and the Republican campaign committee. I could not have imagined the hundreds of unique opportunities that I would have to make a difference on the state, national and world stage.

In 1964, west-side Indianapolis neighbors of our factory asked me to run as one of seven candidates on a Citizens School Committee slate in the 1964 citywide election. I had never considered running for the School Board and did not want to do so then. Brother Tom and I were beginning to make profitable headway, and I was eager to enjoy several more years of such activity on our business ventures.

The death of President Kennedy affected all of us. For my wife, Charlene, and me it meant taking stock of what we were doing and a quickening of conscience. Char's basic instincts and priorities have always been unerring. I entered the school board election, which was filled with all of the turmoil surrounding a partisan campaign in our community. The period of service after victory was commenced with sit-ins and occupations of the school board offices, and deeply controversial agendas as we tried to make headway against racial discrimination, severe under achievement in many inner-city schools, the proper role of state and federal governments in local school governance, and other heady dilemmas. Meanwhile, I felt an emotional involvement with public school pupils and teachers.

Service on the school board unexpectedly led some Republicans to come and ask me to run for mayor of Indianapolis. Until that time, I had never had an interest in the work of a mayor. However, during the fall of 1966, my interest became intense. In January 1967, I announced I would run and the bid that November was successful. After eight years on the job, and one unsuccessful statewide run, I was elected to the U.S. Senate, in 1976.

These years of public service have been filled with remarkable changes and improvements for thousands. The access to people, to information, and to ideas provides enormous opportunities to think and to act. The rewards from improving people's lives are countless.

Larry's own story and the others he tells are an inspiration for all seeking to find their place, and work, in life. Building on his missionary zeal, and his skills as a teacher, Larry became the all-American crusading newspaper editor.

His achievements have been many and great. From prison reform to education, from school desegregation to mental illness, Larry has used the courage of his convictions to force needed changes.

Larry's work represents the hope and challenge of democracy, not just in the United States of America, but around the world. Larry has proven democracy can deliver hope to individuals in need. And by tackling a myriad of social challenges, he has shown that a dedicated individual can make a difference for the better.

For those of us in public service, Larry stands as a beacon for the next generations to follow.

My hope is that some of the zest Larry and I have for getting involved and making a difference rubs off on the reader of this book. Anyone stepping forward will need to push through the tens of barriers that get in the way. If we are not discouraged, those challenges seem always to be overcome. Larry's book inspires the ideas that will help serve us all and the dreams that offset the time and tedium of waiting for those great moments and eventual success.

Ratliff family album

Innocents, Donna Ratliff (right),
Tammy (center) and Jamie

Chapter One

DONNA

I was sorely tempted to say, "You little shit, you're finally getting out of prison so stop your whining."

Big deal that Superintendent Blank wouldn't let her friend pick her up for the drive to the women's shelter in Fort Wayne.

Here was the girl whose grit had proved that given a decent chance, a violent young offender could transform tragedy into triumph. But she wasn't about to celebrate. No, now she just sounded like an old grump.

It was my last visit with Donna Ratliff at the Indiana Women's Prison. Just two weeks more and she'd leave the grim brick buildings of America's oldest prison for women behind her. Granted the scene in the visitor's room didn't inspire celebration.

A chubby African-American guard looked on with nonchalance from the other side of the glass partition as we sat in the drab, cream-colored visitors' room. I guessed the guard was at the end of her shift.

At the other end of the room, near two monster vending machines, a family watched their little girl crawl up and down on one of the red plastic chairs. They seemed to have nothing to say to each other. Being together, I guessed, was the point.

One thing about Donna's foul mood. It matched the drizzle in central Indiana that day. Now you saw her darker side, petty, self-centered, moody. On such occasions, her voice lapsed into a drawl that reminded me of her family's Kentucky roots. I shook off my impulse to scold.

Instead, I patted her on the shoulder. I told her the complaining probably had more to do with her fear of this big change than how she'd make the two-hour trip to the Fort Wayne shelter.

"Of course I'm scared," she shot back. Her eyes clouded with tears. She seemed honked off at me for stating the obvious, as if I had just noted she was wearing a grey sweatshirt with jeans and that her pretty brown hair covered her neck.

When Donna was 14, she set fire to her family home in Huntington. Her mother Glissie and her 16-year-old sister Jamie died in the fire. Smoke inhalation killed them, the medical examiner recorded.

The state placed Donna in an adult prison. Never mind her age. Never mind all the abuse she had suffered in that family. Never mind her desperate need for therapy to sort out a host of psychological problems.

"My crime was big," Donna once said, offering the only plausible reason the Huntington court came down so hard on her and why she ended up in an adult prison. She had no clue, of course, how angry the plight of an abused child in an adult prison would make so many people.

Her case got prominent billing on the front page of The New York Times, her sad young face startling readers nationwide one December morning. She could have been a child in a third-world country, her eyes begging for an American sponsor.

Newspapers around the country picked up the story. It was featured in an hour-long production, "If I Get Out Alive," for National Public Radio. It also got told on cable network talk shows.

She had been locked up for seven often troubled years. During all that time, she struggled with depression. She thought of suicide. Her eating disorder kept coming back. She had nightmares, awakening to cry out for "Mommy." She feared getting beaten up. She fretted nobody loved her.

People in Huntington thought she got off easy. After all, her sentence called for only 25 years when the judge could have sentenced her to 60. Her dad and an older sister, living in Kentucky, demanded she get the maximum.

She did get a better deal than it sounded, which had little to do with the judge's mercy. In Indiana, one day of good behavior counts as two toward your sentence. They knock off a few years if you attend counseling, get a high school diploma and a college degree. Donna had done all that.

Even before my last visit, she had asked me not to show up for her exit from the prison. I surmised that she didn't want me on hand to record the event. I didn't press the matter. After all my editorials and columns about her, I guessed she worried I'd write her release up for the newspaper, and that would have brought unwanted attention to her presence at her new residence.

Nevertheless, I could picture her departure.

She'd give everyone she knew a hug. Yes, the guards, too. That's how it was three years earlier when an appeals court ordered her sent to a juvenile treatment center and she was transferred to such a center in Fort Wayne. This young killer never passed a friend who hadn't earned a hug.

You can bet, too, that on the day of her release, her blue eyes would dart back and forth toward other inmates who stood in line to wish her well. Forever this girl was on the hunt for affirmation.

In her final moments, she would hurriedly collect the cardboard box of her belongings at the administration building. That would include her biggest prize, a framed Bachelor of General Studies diploma from Ball State University. Then, she'd sign papers that listed her new address, finally toting the box to the waiting van.

One hundred and twenty miles north, women at the shelter would be on hand to greet this notorious newcomer. Somebody would help her unpack and get settled in her spartan second-floor quarters.

For the first time since May 8, 1995, the day of the fire when she was 14, nobody else would decide when she had to go to bed, when she'd get up and how she'd spend her waking moments.

Every time I think of Donna, despite all she's overcome, I still find myself feeling sorry for the girl. All the hours I spent with her, on the phone, at the prison, in the juvenile center, interviewing her, taping her voice, offering encouragement when she shared her problems, I never could shake the awareness of the tragedy, what happened to her and what horrors she had brought upon the family.

I'll never forget the sad smiles of Donna's mother in old photographs, the downright weird talks I had with her dad, Perry, and the upbeat probation report on her sister Jamie just days before her death.

Nine years after the fire, Donna still must find the memories painful. Despite it all, she overcame so much. She proved her critics cruelly wrong. She made her advocates proud. Yet freed from prison, she will forever be the prisoner of her crime.

I haven't heard much from Donna since her release. I've seen her a couple of times. She seems happy. I'm thankful for that. She's more than justified the faith so many people had placed in her. For now, though, she's through with my nosy questions. As if I hadn't plumbed the depths and more of her story anyway.

In addition to my visits with Donna, I enlisted attorneys, clergy and others to her cause. I talked lawmakers into introducing bills to separate juvenile offenders from adults. I made Donna the poster child for the cause, the injustice of locking kids up with hardened adult criminals.

Now she will bear a new identity, a free woman. It's hard to believe because even to this day I think of her as just the mixed-up, frightened kid from Huntington. You could argue she had earned the right to melt into the anonymity of a big city and not be some journalist's latest project.

But as she told me many times, maybe if I told her story, it would help some other kid in adult-sized trouble. Which is why Donna belongs in this book.

Chapter Two

TO BE OF USE

If the story of my quarter century writing editorials and columns for the Fort Wayne Journal Gazette amounts to a hill of beans, that's because it shows how a newspaper can prod ordinary citizens to change the world.

Just a few years after my retirement from the paper, I'm still amazed and humbled at the reforms I used the editorials to help bring about. School children no longer are paddled. City schools are racially integrated. A troubled teenager was moved from prison to a juvenile treatment center. Programs were created to bring those with mental illness into the mainstream.

My creed goes like this. Anybody can fight city hall and win a round or two. Anybody can join the struggle for justice. Anybody make his or her life count for something. Anybody can be his or her brother and sister's keeper.

Right off the bat, I concede this. I enjoyed an edge over most activists. I got to broadcast my calls for reform from the editorial pages of a major daily newspaper. But even the changes I coaxed along took a lot more than passionate editorials to get the job done.

Answering the paper's call to action, ordinary citizens wrote letters to the editor. They knocked on the governor's door. They filed lawsuits. They pestered lawmakers with e-mails and telephone calls. They joined hands with their neighbors, marched for peace and signed petitions that demanded reform.

Many learned how to enlist the newspaper in their battles. (In ways such as camping outside my office until I listened to their story.)

For me, a born do-gooder and unrepentant bleeding heart, writing editorials turned out to be the best job in town. I like to write. An only child, I'm self-centered enough to think that my opinions matter—or ought to. They not only paid me for this work. The Journal Gazette's owners and the editors let me do my thing.

I took up unpopular causes. "Champion of the underdog," the late Republican state Sen. Charles "Bud" Meeks called me. A Chicago writer who had worked at my paper years ago used to say I was the city's conscience.

Such characterizations flattered me. While they give me too much credit for what always was a team effort, I did work hard to make myself heard.

I offered advice to readers on every subject from negotiations for Mideast peace to the regulation of ice cream vending trucks. I got personally involved. (I know, journalists aren't supposed to do that, but I believe editorial writers and columnists miss the boat if they don't.)

I had spent a few years as a high school English teacher, and developed unorthodox views on teaching. Naturally, these views I passed along in editorials at a time school reform had become a hot topic. (I found out people can get pretty worked up about school matters. Gov. Bob Orr, whose 1980s education reforms I had criticized, tried to get me fired.)

As a journalist, I enjoyed terrific access to those in power. U.S. senators and the state's governors returned calls. Political candidates of every stripe dropped by my office to visit. National experts on child abuse, school desegregation, juvenile justice and a host of other issues took the time to tutor me. Often phone conversations with these people lasted more than an hour. College and graduate school rarely were so edifying.

Doors opened everywhere. I met scores of other experts at conferences for editorialists and education writers. As president of the Education Writers Association and as ethics chairman for the National Conference of Editorial Writers, I helped plan conferences.

I traveled widely with other journalists, and the trips to far-away lands filled me with wonder.

One chilly April afternoon, I found myself in a bunker atop the Golan Heights, looking down on Syrian guns in the lush, green Bekaa Valley below. A decade later, in the summer heat, I stood by the remnants of the Berlin Wall as a muscular young German chiseled out a piece of rock from the wall I could take home as a souvenir.

I wiped tears from my eyes as I huddled with others in a drab Prague flat to witness an elderly Czech woman, a shut-in, vote in her country's first free elections in 44 years. Again and again in Eastern Europe, I met ordinary people who had challenged old tyrannies and injustice. (Compared to them, I ranked as a mere amateur in the activist business.)

In 1992, my wife Toni and I lived in Washington, D.C. She had a one-year appointment at the National Science Foundation. Meantime, I wrote editorials from the paper's bureau in the National Press Building, near the White House. It was one of the most exciting years of my life. I interviewed presidents of other countries, members of Congress and cabinet secretaries. I attended lectures at the Smithsonian.

In turn, a reporter interviewed me for the Voice of America to be broadcast, with a voice-over, throughout the Russian republics. When I got off the phone, I confessed to our bureau editor, Sylvia Smith, that I was so nervous I had no idea what I had just said.

After our sojourn in the nation's capital, I plugged away at grassroots reform in Fort Wayne. There, once more, I watched ordinary people transcend their prejudices and set aside their differences with others to support a good cause.

If I helped change the lives of children and others in our community for the better, my job changed me. It made me less self-centered. It taught me to be more flexible. It forced me to honor the goodness in those I disagreed with. It inspired me to extend myself as a friend to those who were hurting.

I had the great good fortune to work with highly intelligent, scrupulously honest and caring colleagues. Associating with them made me a better writer and a more effective advocate.

The reforms people accomplished during my watch likely will extend far beyond my life and that of my contemporaries. My side's causes didn't always prevail—strict gun control and a ban on the death penalty, to name a couple that fizzled. I don't consider them lost causes at all. It's just business that awaits the attention of my successors.

Each crusade I got involved in had its own heroes and villains. Each produced real, vintage Hoosier characters. At times, each seemed like a lost cause if ever there was one. Those moments arrived just when I had become most smug about the rightness of the cause.

But on the whole, in this age of bad news, I've got a book of good news. When the articles on the front page tempt us to despair, I have a story of hope.

Family album

With my wife Toni Kring

Chapter Three

RAY AND GERTIE

It's always bothered me to see somebody getting mistreated. Like Holden Caulfield in J.D. Salinger's *Catcher in the Rye*, I thought of myself as the protector of children.

But for all the sensitivity I felt toward others' suffering, it took me a lot of years to develop into a social reformer. Caring isn't necessarily followed by doing.

When I did start speaking out, in my college years, I did so with too much ego and too little wisdom to make a difference. I was like that first sea creature that awoke dazed to find itself on dry land without fins. It takes a while to figure out what you've become and how you're supposed to act.

Early influences counted for a lot. So I should say a few words about my being a kid and what came shortly after.

The kid part was spent mostly during the 1940s back in Defiance, Ohio, a college town of 10,000 straddling the muddy Auglaize and equally muddy Maumee rivers in Republican northwest Ohio.

People worked at such places as Defiance Screw Machine Works, the Coke plant, Arps Dairy, which supplied the milk I grew up on, Brown's Bakery, whose owner rented us the corner duplex we lived in, Willie-Garman Auto Supply, where Dad worked for a few years, Kuntz's drugs, neighborhood bars like Catarino's a block from our house, Pixler's Clothes, where we bought my scout uniforms, and the county courthouse where, as a kid, I had no clue of what went on.

An only child, I often found myself alone. This solitude gave me a life rich with imaginings, some wondrous, some grandiose, others spooky like the recurring one in which Gypsies kidnapped me.

If nobody came by to play, I'd bounce a scruffy old baseball off the porch steps. When I was about 12 or 13, I'd take my prize rod and reel and practice casting a lead sinker in the side yard. (I was nuts about fishing.) I'd often sing, lowering my voice to crooner range, imitating Bing Crosby. (Years later, a director of the funeral home across the street would remind me of my singing.)

Such framed many weeks in the summer. I also found time to hang out at the Kettenring Country Club, east of Defiance. In 1944, Dad beat out my best friend Davy's dad in a sudden-death playoff for the club's golf championship.

Winters found my ear glued to our big mahogany radio in the living room as the Green Hornet and Sergeant Preston of the Yukon tracked down bad guys. I also shot a fair amount of pool at the Elks Club, half a block from our house.

In the fall, football was my passion. In those days a game in my yard meant tackling until I broke Davy Morehouse's collarbone. We were in the first grade. Lacking a game, I'd hike a couple of blocks to downtown and Defiance's lively Clinton Street, our small town bazaar in post-World War II America.

A favorite stop was the B.F. Goodrich store. For months, I was obsessed with a red Schwinn bike there. To my uncontainable joy at age eight, it showed up at our house, 602 Jefferson, on Easter. Thank you, risen Jesus.

At Christmas, the store had model train displays. Homework could wait that time of year. I loved to watch the model trains with the engines that coughed out tiny puffs of smoke and livestock cars that allowed little plastic cattle to wriggle around an attached platform.

In the spring one year, Ernie McGinness, the B.F. Goodrich manager, let me play hooky and took me to the Auglaize to fish. Occasionally, Ernie would pass me the cask of homemade wine so I could keep warm as we waited for the stupid catfish to bite.

Ray and Gertie were my dad and mom. He drove a Coke truck, and during the Good War, assembled radios for the army. He had lots of other jobs, though always drifting back to machine shops. For a while, he sold Kirby vacuum sweepers door to door and liked to take me along on his calls. (Dad had the charm to make it as a salesman but had trouble getting his butt off the bar stool to follow up leads.)

Until cancer brought him low in his late 50s, he was a survivor. I'll give you a good example. During a house call on a chilly fall afternoon, he meant to show this woman how tough the

24

Kirby attachments were. So he slammed a plastic tube on the floor. "Thwack!" went the tube against the beige carpet, and "klunk" went the half that had broken off against the ceiling. Without so much as an apology for the dent in the woman's ceiling, he calmly explained that the attachment had been in the cold car and understandably was brittle.

I stared in wonderment as Dad wrote up the sales order for the smiling and grateful woman.

His greatest display of tenacity came into play when he spent three years after their divorce coaxing Mom to marrying him again. When she finally relented, and they again tied the knot with me, their 15-year-old son, looking on, he continued the drinking, gambling and golfing obsessions that drove her to divorce him in the first place. (It probably has nothing to do with genetics that my wife calls me the most persistent person she ever met.)

It's not easy to grow up with a father who has a drinking problem. It wasn't the physical abuse when he had too much to drink. I don't recall any of that. For me, it was the embarrassment. You want so bad to be proud of your dad. Most of the time, I was. People liked him. Girls in my class said he was handsome. He could be pals with me, teaching me to play golf, taking me to movies.

But after a few drinks, he turned into a boisterous, argumentative jerk who would make a scene at a restaurant. His steak wasn't rare enough to suit him or the service was too slow, and he'd make a noisy fuss. I hated such moments. They made me hugely ashamed, and I prayed none of my friends heard about Dad's behavior. Sadly, he just couldn't keep his promises to stop drinking.

Like Dad, Mom loved to party. She went to work full-time when I was pretty young. She might well have been the greatest secretary there ever was. When it came to typing, she had no peer. Her fingers flew over the keys so fast you couldn't see which ones she'd just struck. She took shorthand and translated a judge or attorney's stilted boilerplate into plain English. Mom answered the phones with charm. Among friends and relatives alike, her people skills were legendary. She could have developed rapport with a department store mannequin.

"My favorite aunt," every cousin called her. She worked at the First Federal Savings & Loan in Defiance, for "a short time," she recalled. They gave her a little cream-colored bank for me and I put dimes in it for the Christmas Club.

Years later, she ran an accounting office in Fort Wayne. I doubt if she shrank from issuing bold directives to the accountants as well as the office girls. She would be heard. She was the youngest in her family, the spoiled and favored sibling. It gave her an entitlement she exercised until her death at 91. By then, even though her brain had become a tangle of Alzheimer's neurons, she still was barking orders at the nurses who passed by her room at the nursing home.

If Mom could be bossy, Dad loved to argue. The subject didn't matter. He had lots of opinions, all negative, about Democrats in general and the Roosevelts in particular, though he guessed it was OK the Democrats won the war. He pooh-poohed the fears of a Communist takeover, but he wasn't sure about the pope's intentions for America.

Herbert Hoover was not a dirty word in our family. At least not with Dad. His heroes included Barry Goldwater. I think it was Barry's blunt way of speaking that Dad liked. His world view put him at odds with organized labor. Yet he benefited from the labor movement, an irony he didn't appreciate. After all, as a non-union tool-and-die maker, the career he settled into, he earned the good wages unions had won in their shops before. But he refused to join on the grounds that unions protected incompetent or lazy workers. I recall he didn't like Walter Reuther or John L. Lewis, powerful labor leaders of that day.

Dad just had those beliefs, and if I pressed him, he'd get sore as if I were dumb for asking.

I had plenty of quarrels with Mom and Dad's parenting. Even as a kid who suffered nothing of real child abuse, I protested, to no avail, Dad's dumb ritual on my birthday. Before the cake and ice cream appeared on the table, and I made my wish, he'd take me into the living room and order me to bend over one arm of our brown couch. He'd give me one whack for every year, then an extra whack, "to grow on," he said.

I was 12 when he gave up this ridiculous business.

I also hated that he yelled "Butterfingers!" every time I dropped a ball he'd thrown to me. Here I balance his ridicule against the fact that he did, after all, play a great deal of catch with me; in his mind, he was grooming me to be a big league baseball pitcher. His ambitions, however, left my talents in the dust by 100 miles. Nevertheless, he taught me to dream the impossible dream.

As I grew older, I came to understand Dad battled his own demons. There was the death of his younger brother when they were barely more than adolescents. There was the regret that as "the smartest in the class," he didn't go to college.

Mom could be strict. She had no patience with my "back talk," an affliction I absolutely had no control over. I just naturally questioned authority, including hers. She would order me to sit in a chair or crack me a good one on my skull with her thimbled forefinger, which left a stinging sensation for minutes.

Yet I warmly recall Mom joining me each Sunday evening to listen to classic radio programs, such as "The Jack Benny Show" and "Lux Radio Theater." She would bring out left-over roast beef from Sunday dinner and make sandwiches lathered with real butter, and we'd eat over a card table in the living room. Dad, likely as not, would be playing cards with his cronies.

I never heard them talk of social reform, ending injustice or fighting city hall. That hardly made them exceptional among their friends. But if they indulged racial prejudice, I never saw it. Given the small Ohio towns they grew up in—Dad in Paulding, Mom in Van Wert, hardly liberal bastions—they treated everyone who crossed their path with respect, rich or poor, black or white.

As a high-schooler in Paulding, Dad played basketball with the "colored guys." For a year or so, we lived in Latty, a hamlet in Paulding County. Our house was just across the railroad from his parents' home. In Latty, Dad enjoyed cordial relations with the black families. They all seemed to know him, and feel warmly toward him, I gathered, from his school days in the county seat.

I can't imagine Mom, the preeminent people person, being rude or thinking unkindly toward somebody because of the person's race, religious beliefs or ethnic background. (She did have plenty of beefs with certain people, though.) You might say she was a practicing humanist, small "h."

If Dad had thought much at all about race, he not only would have said racial prejudice was cruel. He also would have said it was stupid. That was his word for you when he didn't feel like arguing. "Case closed," he'd say.

It bothered him to see anyone mistreated. He liked to boast that he was "pulling for the underdog." That didn't just apply to his favorite sports teams, such as the Red Sox and Dallas Cowboys. Meeting somebody a bit slow or disabled or somebody getting a raw deal pained him. He'd shake his head and say,

"What a damn shame." On injustices, though on little else, Mom shared Dad's opinion.

It was Dad who inspired me to look with compassion on the downtrodden. He would denounce those who mistreated others. He'd lecture me on what was fair and just. If he occasionally caused me grief when I was a kid, I owe him a debt for showing me that it's a good thing to care about the weakest among us. Long ago, I forgave him for the other stuff. Mom, too.

Family album

That handsome couple, Ray and Gertie,
who were my parents

Chapter Four

BOY PREACHER

I know exactly where I got the idea to be a preacher. (This is also the beginning of the social reformer part.)

That I trace to Dad's parents in Latty, Ohio, Mom and Tom Hayes, as we all called them. (One of their quirks: They didn't want to be Grandpa and Grandma. The preference never struck me as odd.)

I saw Mom's warm and kindly parents infrequently. They lived in Van Wert, Ohio. For us in Defiance, that was a half hour's drive beyond Latty in our faded black '37 Plymouth coupe. I loved Jessie and Grace, but Dad's folks lived closer and gave me a second set of parents.

In the summers, I spent weeks at a time with them. That proved to be a refuge from my parents' chronic battles in which ashtrays and hateful words punctuated the air for as long as I could remember. (During those times at home, I retreated to my bedroom and fiddled with the parachute jump I made with my Gilbert's Erector set or glued a balsa wood wing to a model airplane.)

At Mom and Tom's, life got predictable. You knew everything that was going to happen. You knew what we'd have for breakfast, lunch and supper. You knew what time Floyd and Emma Baxter were coming over to play pinochle. You knew that Mom Hayes would smear the popcorn with margarine. And earlier in the day, you knew what time her Detroit Tigers with Harry Heilmann announcing were coming on.

People today say kids need structure. Well, I sure had it in Latty.

Middays it was Paul Harvey and the news; Sundays, her radio preachers. (The Methodist Church in town didn't baptize by immersion or observe weekly communion like the Church of Christ in the county seat of Paulding. So Mom and Tom skipped services. But they did let the Methodists have a go at me for vacation Bible school.)

At breakfast, as sunlight danced off the flowered wallpaper, they schooled me in the editorial pages of The Journal Gazette and got me started in what would become my lifelong practice of debating the columnists over the shredded wheat and jelly-covered wheat toast.

Long before I learned to read, Mom Hayes read to me—Bible stories. She had me memorize the names of all the books of the Bible. After I learned to read, she had me memorize long passages, from Genesis, Acts, Romans and 1 Corinthians. So it was that she hooked me forever on the stately cadences of the King James Bible. (Even today, I prefer it to modern translations.)

She recounted the visits of Church of Christ evangelists who held revival meetings in the county. She recalled high points of sermons and cited the numbers who "came forward to accept Christ and be baptized" from one night to the next. These things she shared; family scandals—and we had a few I would learn later—she kept to herself.

One high point of those homemade Sunday School sessions came when she'd reach into the oaken cabinet next to her bed and pull out yellowed paper that had a sermon my great-grandfather, the Reverend John W. Hayes, had written on. (I was by no means the first writer in the family.)

I don't recall the theological points. What sticks were the illustrations, always about the goodness of some biblical character or a guy he met in his travels, helping to start new Churches of Christ in Ohio, Indiana and Michigan. Clearly, Rev. Hayes loved people. My grandmother also said he was a lousy farmer, lest I think anybody on my grandfather's side was lacking in faults.

Tutoring me in this family church lore, Mom Hayes planted in my mind the idea that someday I'd become a minister. Indeed, when a young minister from southern Illinois named Bob Hargrave came to Defiance, my home town, and organized a Church of Christ, he quickly picked up on my family-nurtured interest in the ministry.

He squired me to church meetings and youth rallies around the area. Once, he and I drove all the way from Defiance to Lincoln, Illinois, where he had attended a Christian college for graduate school. Bob had me deliver my first sermon at age 12. My topic was, "Love is the greatest thing in the world." After we moved to Fort Wayne when I was in high school, another young minister, Bill Lower, assumed my mentorship. Bill enlisted me to read Scripture, to lead the singing and, a few times, to preach during evening services.

When I graduated from high school, I enrolled in his alma mater, a tiny religious school in central Michigan, Great Lakes Christian College. (Lower had been the school's first graduate.) Even Mom and Tom crowded into Dad's 1954 red Buick Century with me and my folks to make the trip to those old stone-covered farm buildings on the 80-acre campus. So it was that they all launched me on one of my life's missions.

But years later, more secular voices would summon me to other missions of consequence.

Family album

Mom and Tom Hayes surveying their Latty domain

Chapter Five

BIBLE YEARS

You wouldn't think of a Bible college, of fundamentalist bent, as a place to learn to question authority or to think for yourself. But my stint in such a school did nurture my questioning spirit. That would serve me well years later as an editorial writer.

I don't know about Bible colleges of other traditions. In the 1950s, Great Lakes Christian College was no cloistered, regimented institution where grim-faced professors indoctrinated young students in a strict ideology no one dared question.

Off campus, in our cabin on Rock Lake, we huddled under blankets next to the one stove in our cabin as we tested our beliefs against the logic of others. Granted, our arguments sometimes veered from the sensible to the silly. For example, Don Koke and I once debated into the night whether one could be legitimately baptized in milk, as opposed to water.

Of course, we all believed in the Bible—all 47 of us who were enrolled on the sandy shrub-littered Michigan campus my freshman year. But fellow students and I had big arguments about why Jesus' cleansing of the temple occurred at the beginning of his ministry in the Gospel of John and at the end of his ministry in the other three.

We didn't bother to debate social issues. Which, now that I think about it, is odd. After all, I enrolled at Great Lakes at the dawn of the civil rights movement, just a couple of years after the Brown decision. Nobody objected. I heard none of the right-wing complaints about Chief Justice Earl Warren that became so much a part of evangelicals' mantra a few years later.

In fact, my recollection is that everybody treated our few black students as equals. One of these students often took white students to visit her minister father's nearby black church.

The professors, who often served as ministers in nearby churches, welcomed theological questions. I never felt put down or belittled for my impertinent challenges to received doctrine. To the contrary, I got the impression the profs rather enjoyed the chance to display their scholarship.

If conservative, the biblical scholarship was first rate. I recall Lee Doty, dean of the college, with great fondness. No fuddy-duddy, a clown at summer church camp, he expected you to work your tail off in class.

Lee introduced us to the world of modern biblical scholarship. Although he rejected the critics' conclusions, he presented those views fairly. He told us about the theory that Moses wasn't the author of the first five books of the Bible. It was multiple authors, writing over a period of centuries.

If Lee hadn't introduced us to such theories, it wouldn't have occurred to me to question the authorship of any of the books of the Bible.

Professor Jim Greenwood pushed us so hard in Greek class that most of the guys dropped out after the first quarter. Only my roommate Bud Downs and I survived to make it to second-year Greek. All the while, we had a lot of fun competing with each other and showing off our grasp of Greek verb conjugations.

If you like innovative teaching methods, how's this? Glen Waterson, who mainly served as our speech and homiletics professor, offered a course in logic. No philosopher by training, he got thrown for a loop by a couple of students over one problem after another in our textbook. At the end of the hour, he would look nonplussed.

After a few weeks of this, which embarrassed this kind man, he moved his seat back with the students. Without saying it, he signaled that we'd all teach the class, and he'd just be one of the students. So we took turns explaining our theories about how to solve problems the text posed.

Weekends, with the professors gone, we moved the folding chairs in the chapel aside and danced as the musically gifted Ed Erskine played show tunes on the chapel piano that only days before had accompanied us to "Amazing Grace" and "Blessed Assurance."

If you got caught drinking, you would have been kicked out. Or if you got caught having sex you could have been dismissed, too. I was aware, however, that lots of heavy necking went on under the coats in the back of our touring choir bus. But if that had been found out, it would have drawn no more than a reprimand.

About everybody who showed up at such a school would

have been a straight arrow. I only flirted with being an exception, as one incident suffices to illustrate.

John Sears, a minister who taught English and was the epitome of a gentleman, summoned me for a private meeting. He wasn't the only bald prof, but he was the only one with a neatly trimmed mustache and rimless glasses.

We met at the counter in the front office. With his head down, his voice lowered, he told me how disappointed he was to hear that I had been smoking off campus. Oh was I guilty. (So much for peppermint oil covering up the tobacco smell.) Professor Sears' talk didn't make me quit. But I sure felt like a jerk.

When the college celebrated its 50th anniversary many years later, I joined my old classmates for an emotional reunion in Lansing where the school had moved in the middle of my junior year.

For the Sunday service in the chapel, I jumped at the chance to sing in the alumni choir. If people knew I had left the Church of Christ and college's views of the Bible, they never asked me to defend myself. Nor did anybody shun me because I had become a Unitarian and had made no secret of my apostasy.

I couldn't begin to describe the gulf between my old friends who remain evangelicals and myself. It stretches from Genesis to the book of Revelation, from right-wing Republican politics to left-wing Democratic.

Further, polls suggest that an evangelical opposes abortion, gun control and sex education in the schools while religious liberals hold contrary opinions. Yet I know the stereotypes don't necessarily hold.

The truth is those folk who take the Bible literally can be just as thoughtful, fair-minded and compassionate as your card-carrying liberal. I wouldn't think of ridiculing them. Once upon a time, they were my classmates and among the dearest of friends. They tolerated my dissents and let me think for myself. They remain my friends.

Chapter Six

APOSTASY

I flopped as a fundamentalist. And as a heretic, I proved to be no quick study. It was trial and error and aggravating people whose respect I sought.

In June, 1960, when I picked up my bachelor's degree in religion from Great Lakes, I still had every intention of being a preacher. Or a professor in a theological school.

Great Lakes was one of about 50 small Bible colleges affiliated with the independent Church of Christ or Christian Church. The schools trained preachers and other church workers for this brotherhood's congregations, representing a big chunk of America's largest indigenous religious movement, launched in the 1800s by the Scotch Presbyterian, Alexander Campbell. (That movement today also finds its expression in the non-instrumental Church of Christ and the more liberal Disciples of Christ.)

Campbell, one of the notable religious reformers of the 19th century, influenced by the philosopher John Locke, often showed up on the debate circuit. He took on the luminaries of the day, including scholars from other churches and the socialist Robert Owen. So the school I was graduating from, though founded in the late 1940s and small even by Bible college standards, could point to proud heritage.

Family members and friends of the college crowded into the cinder block church in west Lansing where the graduation ceremony was held. Even Joanie, my girlfriend and a speech major at Central Michigan University, showed up. Embers of that romance had sputtered away, though. By then, I had commenced a weekend ministry in Redkey, Indiana. First college degree in our immediate family. I thought I was pretty hot stuff, as Dad observed.

He didn't mean it to flatter me.

After the service, I irritated the devil out of everybody by trying to arrange the seating at Lights, a favorite north side restaurant in Lansing. Throughout dinner, while I enjoyed the conversation, I had this feeling that I needed to move away from the world of my friends. I look back on that night as a major turning point in my evolution from evangelical preacher and half-baked theologian to liberal social reformer.

By the time the fall rolled around, I had left Great Lakes behind. I enrolled in the Cincinnati Bible Seminary to work toward a graduate divinity degree. This is a much older school, established in the 1920s. The faculty roster included scholars with degrees from Harvard, Yale and Hebrew Union College. Set on a hill overlooking the Ohio River, with a cluster of ivy-covered buildings among newer structures in the city's Price Hill district, the school belonged in another era, another age. So the school had lots of tradition of its own. Not much modern theology here.

Yet it was a congenial campus. On mornings when the air was still, the smell of coffee from a processing plant in the valley below greeted you as you stepped outside your dorm. Students, graduate or undergraduate, made you their instant friend. That I welcomed. In other respects, though, I didn't fit the mold.

In classes, I continued to question my professors' arguments. That wasn't as welcome as it had been at Great Lakes. Worse, I let it slip out that I had some doubts about the conservative view of the Bible. Despite that, in my early years at the school, I still didn't stray far from the fold or that fellowship's basic beliefs.

I was trying out the role of skeptic, to see about the fit. By no stretch would you call my divinity thesis, on the Gospel of John, the product of a religious liberal or social reformer.

Still, I often found myself backing away from old notions presented as irrefutable biblical doctrine. As the days wound down in graduate school, I concluded evolution probably was compatible with Christian faith.

Taking issue with my professors, I argued that the Supreme Court's decisions on prayer and Bible reading in public schools, which came in successive years, were decided correctly on the basis of the U.S. Constitution. Besides, I couldn't imagine how those rulings posed a threat to religion.

It was during the seminary years I married Wanda Hale, an editor of Sunday school literature for Standard Publishing and a fellow graduate student. She was a woman of high intelligence and great faith. In her own quiet, respectful way, she too had raised questions about the school's orthodoxy, a fact I made note of even before we dated.

As I finished my studies, she continued her editing job and picked up free-lance writing assignments, too. Although Wanda didn't go as far with her doubts as I did, she tolerated my growing skepticism. This got a boost from three things.

One was my friendship with Jim Stuart. He had finished his studies at the seminary and then started working on his Ph.D. in philosophy at the University of Cincinnati.

Weekdays, as our wives toiled away in offices to pay the bills, we two graduate students chewed over issues of religion and philosophy at the Hitching Post restaurant on Cincinnati's Glenway Avenue. The 85-cent child's portion of chicken gave you a breast, drumstick and plenty of fries, "my usual." (Even then, I was obsessed with routine.)

With classes out of the way for the day and with only reading to do and papers to write, the familiar meal and the break inspired one to think deep thoughts. At least we thought they were deep. We also scoffed at some things our seminary professors believed and how they taught. We did hold a couple of profs in high regard. One was T.G. Burks, the seminary's philosophy professor. He sometimes joined Jim and me for lunch.

He encouraged students to ask questions and to justify their opinions. No surprise, he had been at odds himself with the seminary's old guard. Professor Burks made a point of telling students they didn't need to check their brains at the door when they enrolled. Such a view of students made Burks a welcome addition to our luncheons.

Professor Burks wasn't around when Jim brought up a question one day that required more than some philosophical banter. The question was as old as theology. In fact, I had puzzled over it myself. But until Jim brought it up, it hadn't sunk in: How do you reconcile the notion of an all-powerful God with one who is also all-loving, given the existence of evil in the world?

It's Job's conundrum. Or, if you like, John 3:16 ("God so loved the world...") vs. Auschwitz.

Later, when I raised the issue with Professor Burks, he conceded that the problem of evil did pose a challenge to belief in God. But in response he argued that skeptics had no accounting for the existence of good in the world.

"Explain that one," he challenged.

I had no good answers for such paradoxes. If it's a leap of faith to believe in God, it's also a leap of faith to accept the idea of not ever knowing whether a personal God exists. But I knew that sooner or later, I'd have to revise my traditional notions and let it go at that.

Within a short time, I did decide to reject the tribal deity who ran things throughout the Old Testament. I couldn't be a fan of a divine being who ordered Jericho-brand ethnic cleansings and tolerated horrible crimes his favorites committed while zapping those who fell out of favor over the most trivial sin. To top it off, when this deity showed his hand in the New Testament, he threatened you with eternal suffering if your opinions fail to meet some arbitrary standard.

Such a notion doesn't take into account that you might just be too stupid to know the "truth" when you're presented with it. I saw another difficulty with such an extraordinary punishment.

Consider this: After a hundred million years in the lake of everlasting fire, no unbeliever, even the purest of heart, would have paid for his sins.

Reasoning such things to their logical conclusion, I realized hell just didn't make any sense; only a god of unimaginable meanness could inflict such suffering on just about anybody.

To be sure, a radically different divine persona makes an occasional appearance in the Old Testament. I'm thinking of the 23rd Psalm and the book of Hosea. We meet this God more frequently in the New Testament.

If there is a Supreme Being, I figure this would be the person with the still, small voice, the one who loves you no matter what, the one with a Carl F. Rogers "unconditional positive regard" way of dealing with folk. (My theology took this turn, I suppose, because I was reading a lot by the humanistic psychologists like Rogers during this time.)

The deity that did make sense didn't jump on your case when you screwed up. His or her voice only occasionally broke into your thoughts. It was when things seemed dark and you needed cheering up.

He or she wasn't apt to berate you with long-winded sermons, only gentle reminders to keep plugging away, that life was too short to worry about things you couldn't change or to stay mad for long at your wife or child.

So from the bits and pieces of my studies, and out of the quiet moments when rumors of a transcendent world intruded, I fashioned my own religion, my own god. (I used to chuckle to myself imagining that this Yahweh was as puzzled about the meaning of it all as anybody else.)

Now as to the revolutionary rabbi of the Sermon on the Mount, he was somebody whose teachings a person could follow. Somewhere along the line, I lost interest in the spooky, untouchable guy who startled Mary in the garden and waltzed through doors to greet his distraught disciples after his execution. My more earthly Jesus, who bit his nails and fantasized about getting laid, wouldn't do at the seminary, of course.

For some reason I won't try to explain, I still get chills of a mystical sort when I listen to a recording of the Mormon Tabernacle Choir perform "The Holy City," one of many numbers we sang in choir at Great Lakes.

I broke with most folk at the seminary over more than theology. This came from the debate on campus over the civil rights movement. In 1960, when I started my studies at the Cincinnati campus, most everyone at the school was for Nixon in the presidential race. But watching the debates with friends, an English professor, Ron Henderson, and his wife Jerri, I had to say I thought Kennedy beat Nixon.

Then, when Kennedy became president, I cheered his stand on civil rights. He was credited with forcing the integration of Old Miss and the University of Alabama. To my distress at the seminary, civil rights divided students.

Black students—one I recall from Barbados named Rupert Bishop—were passionate about the need for all institutions in society to desegregate. But many white students and some professors, though I guess they were for equal rights, cautioned that it had only been 100 years since slavery and going too fast could trigger a backlash from white people.

I thought that view was nuts. I sided with Rupert and the handful of black students on the campus. But then, I was no stranger to the issue.

I had such good black friends at my grandparents' home in Latty, Ohio, where I spent lazy weeks each summer. When I attended high school there briefly, Carl Goings, an African-American student, and I skipped school to go pheasant hunting. On weekends, we shot at pigeons which inhabited an abandoned grain elevator along the Nickel Plate Railroad tracks. We teamed up playing basketball, too. I often visited his home.

Listen, we were equals. I truly looked up to him.

Meantime, at school in Defiance, I often felt like an underdog myself. I was an anxious, sensitive kid, a target for bullies, of which our school had an abundant supply. In my heart, I sided with other kids getting picked on.

For all Dad's prejudices about the Catholic Church and labor unions, he had no use for racism. His attitude sunk in for me, deep. No wonder that my earliest memories find me stirred with anger and sadness at any sign of prejudice.

One incident of racial bigotry in high school remains vivid. It happened at South Side High School, in Fort Wayne. My family had moved from Ohio to the Indiana city in 1955. I was a junior. New at the school, I was taking an elective art class to flesh out the credits I needed to graduate. A freshman in the class, an African-American boy named James, had befriended me, the mid-year newcomer.

At the time, he was one of the few black kids at the school; most blacks attended Central High. One day, as James and I visited outside Mrs. Fleck's room, a tall white boy I didn't know shouted at James, "Hey, jungle bunny, go back to Africa."

I was shocked and angry at this unprovoked cruelty. Without thinking, I lunged at the kid. His response was to push me down. I started to get up when the band director, who was coming down the hall, ran up to us and broke up the scuffle. But I felt so sorry for James, who stood by mute through the brief melee, looking deeply ashamed.

Then, a half dozen years later, the civil rights debate erupted at the seminary.

For all the good things about the school, the high-caliber faculty, the students' seriousness of purpose, many people just didn't seem to connect on racial injustice. I don't think it was all racial prejudice. One thing about the old-line conservatives there. Decent folk all, they didn't like change. Anyway, more and more, I felt out of place at the school and in the church of my ancestors to which I had dedicated my life.

The final shove from the faith of my fathers came from other graduate students. They were my buddies, all of us too smart for our britches and eager to prove it. With questions popping up so often in classes—nationwide, this was the free-speech 60s—my friends and I started a discussion group. Our doubts made people uneasy in class. So we'd air them elsewhere. We invited the more open-minded profs such as Burks to join us at off-campus apartments.

Word about our group got back to the old guard professors. Our little cabal became topic A at faculty meetings. It got nasty, I gathered. Professors like Burks who encouraged the discussion group were called to task. I recall the nature of the rebuke from our legendary theology professor, George Mark Elliott. He told the profs who backed our group:

"I not only give the students the answers, I tell them what questions to ask."

A classic religious schism developed on the campus. (What mischief had my friends and I set afoot?) By the end of that school year, June, 1964, the trustees advised those faculty members in sympathy with the discussion group their contracts wouldn't be renewed. Those of us in the group were devastated.

That fall, seminary President Perry—Woodrow W.— summoned me to his office.

A splendid development it seemed, or so I thought. Did the old guard figure they might tolerate one moderate in their midst? Fantasies caromed through my brain like steelies in a pinball machine. I assumed Perry had heard about my scholarship and wanted to offer me an adjunct teaching job. It turned out to be a rather brief foray into fantasyland.

Amid his Bible commentaries and collection of coffee mugs and family pictures, Dr. Perry spent an hour or so lecturing me about doubts I had raised at my weekend ministry, then in northern Kentucky. He cited Bible passages in English—passages this up-start student had translated from Greek. He gave me no chance to argue any point. When he finished with one pronouncement, he'd lean back and pause. I was supposed to let his argument sink in.

He had this labored way of speaking that made him sound ponderous yet authoritative. The scene returns with a lot of clarity. I see him, his oversized, white-haired head bobbing, as he lays out the fallacies of my thinking. Finally, I picture him nodding. Then his tiny grey eyes direct my attention to his office door. I am excused to leave.

"I guess I'm not going to be offered a teaching job," I muttered as I stood to leave.

President Perry just glared back.

So it was that my heresy trial ended. No torture. No flames lapping around my feet at the stake. Just a dirty look.

I was too close to finishing my degree to abandon it. So I hung around the school and completed my thesis. But I knew I had no future as a minister in the church or as a professor in one of the church's colleges. Unceremoniously booted off the hallelujah train.

The seminary still sends me solicitations for gifts.

Chapter Seven

ROUTE TO THE PAPER

So I wasn't going to be one of the great evangelical preachers of our time.

I had turned away from the seminary's teachings. No mystery there. But my heart wasn't ready to abandon all that. For a time, I was pretty dejected.

I had joked about building "Hayes Tabernacle" and "Hayes Liberal Theological Seminary." (The liberal part my evangelical pals made up to tease me about pestering professors too much with my questions.) I was half-serious when I dreamed someday of being a "big man in the brotherhood." Realistically, I did plan to be a minister in the Church of Christ or even an instructor in some Christian college.

What was I thinking at this time? Did I actually believe I could keep my doubts to myself and pretend to be a believer before my congregation? No, playing such a game wouldn't wash.

I probably still had some notion of a personal God. But I had gradually concluded that the Bible was more human invention than divine revelation. That didn't add up to a career in the Church of Christ.

My encounter with President Perry ended even those down-to-earth dreams. Now I had to revise my dreams. More-over, the time was upon me when I needed to earn a living.

It was 1965. My daughter Robyn had been conceived. My wife would have to quit her job at Standard Publishing, of course. No maternity leaves in those days. It dawned on me that I was going to have a family to support.

Fortunately, I had already devised an option to the ministry. Before I finished my divinity thesis, I had enrolled at Xavier University to work on a graduate degree in English. I'd be a teacher. It wasn't my first dream. But, more and more, being a teacher looked like a pretty good dream. What's more, it gave me the freedom to be true to my own beliefs.

By graduation in May, when I received a divinity degree from the seminary plus a Master's from Xavier, I had to take stock of what had happened to me and my view of religion. It was a painful time. I was not only discarding things my professors in the Christian schools had taught. I was jettisoning a family identity that extended back five generations.

By the end of the year, I was a father and a religious liberal.

At summer's end, I got a job teaching high school English in Dayton, Kentucky. That went pretty well. I've always loved kids, even teenagers. Most of the kids seemed to like me and the class. Moreover, I had great fun directing the senior class plays.

In pursuit of a better salary—Kentucky teacher salaries were among the lowest in the country then—I landed a teaching job in Milford, Ohio, a suburb east of Cincinnati. School there had barely started when Dad phoned to inform me that he had developed cancer of the colon, possibly fatal.

So to be close to him and Mom, I moved the family to Fort Wayne to teach at my alma mater, South Side High School. Naturally, I carted along my new theological persona, along with progressive ideas about teaching and politics.

Until Wanda and I divorced, we attended the Lincolnshire Church of the Brethren, one of the historic peace churches. But it was only a matter of time before my church home became the city's most liberal church, the Unitarian-Universalist congregation.

In my first year teaching in Fort Wayne, I fell in with the most politically liberal group of teachers. We were the ones who defended students accused of violating the school dress code. We adopted an informal teaching style, after what was known then, using reformer Herb Kohl's language, as the "open classroom." In every way we could, we gave students greater freedom and, we thought, more challenges to learn.

Which wasn't always appreciated by the powers that be.

The best job I had during my public school career came at South Side. That's when I team taught with Ralph Bogardus. He didn't fit the mold. He not only held a teaching degree but a law degree as well. Eventually, he taught American studies at the University of Alabama.

Ralph was a soft-spoken government teacher with curly

blonde hair and wire-rim glasses, the very image of a 60s radical. We selected 20 talented seniors willing to risk a non-traditional classroom. We told them they'd help design the curriculum. We debated political issues, respecting all sides. We studied such novels as Camus' *The Stranger* and Heller's *Catch-22*. Students made slide-tape shows on topics of their choosing, from handwriting analysis to the Holocaust.

Meantime, Ralph introduced me to intellectually challenging reading such as *The New York Review of Books*. He used a Socratic, questioning method to get students to engage topics deeply. He exhibited infinite patience with students' differences of opinions. With his quiet, probing and caring manner, he became a role model for me for all the years I taught in the public schools and, later, as an adjunct professor of writing and peace studies at Indiana University-Purdue University Fort Wayne.

Early in my teaching in Fort Wayne, I let students know I opposed the Vietnam War. That was a minority view among the faculty. But neither criticism of the war nor my unconventional teaching style drew reprimands. Nevertheless, word of my "radical" bent got around. When I was transferred twice to different Fort Wayne Community schools within two years, I got the message.

I never felt I was in danger of losing my job with FWCS. But following Dad's death, I took a year off from teaching to figure out what to do with the rest of my life. I was mentally exhausted. I battled depression.

I just had to reconsider my teaching career. I loved the classroom. But I was out of place among the conservative teachers in the lounge. Of course, with a family to provide for, I needed to find a way to earn a paycheck.

I passed a test to become a mailman. I pumped gas. I ran a lathe in a machine shop. Casting about for something that intrigued me, I went to The Journal Gazette's editor, Larry Allen, to see if he had a writing job for me. As luck would have it, he was looking for someone to add to the editorial page staff. Could I write editorials?

Could I ever. Dad was positively prolific with his opinions. No wonder I grew up spouting opinions on politics and nearly everything else.

It was late summer, 1973. I got off at 3 p.m. from the machine shop and sat down at the IBM Selectric in the managing editor's office. That guy was on vacation. For three hours, with Allen checking in on me periodically, I cranked out 13 snappy editorials on a list of topics he provided, from Spiro Agnew to school desegregation.

A few days later, Allen called to say he'd talked with the publisher Dick Inskeep. They agreed to give me a try part-time. I'd be paid the princely sum of $10 for each editorial. My first piece was unpretentious and its position hardly what you'd call liberal. I merely praised FBI director Clarence Kelly's innovative police patrol when Kelly was the chief in Kansas City, Missouri.

Allen and Inskeep liked that piece and others I wrote for the paper that fall. I don't recall that they rejected any. Just before Christmas, Allen telephoned to let me know I was being hired full-time for the weekly salary of $125. Yes, it wasn't much money, even in that day. It was a fraction of what I had earned teaching school. But I was ecstatic. My friends, joining my family for a Christmas party, applauded what they all agreed was "Larry's true niche."

Chapter Eight

SANTA'S HELPER

Some days it only took a phone call to stir me to crusade mode. One example:

"No Christmas toys for poor kids."

The voice on the other end of the line said a lot more. But I had heard all I needed to. My vision of a Dickens-like Christmas for Fort Wayne's poor children started to take shape. I could see it all, a cold apartment, a half-empty box of Cheerios on the kitchen table. A mother staring vacantly at her coffee, a cigarette hanging loosely from her lips. And more: A joyless child sitting quietly in front of a scrawny Christmas tree decorated with half dozen ornaments and no string of lights.

I scribbled some notes from the call, then rolled a blank sheet of paper into my IBM Selectric and began to tap out an appeal to the good citizens of Fort Wayne to give generously to the Christmas Bureau, lest some poor child not have a Christmas.

I had only been writing editorials for the paper a few months when the fateful call came. I had made sweeping pronouncements on all manner of topics—the plight of the Palestinians, the good news the whooping crane survives, debates between politicians and environmentalists over flood control in this city situated among three rivers, each waterway with a mind of its own.

What I wrote I knew mostly from reading news stories and from phone calls to people mentioned in those stories. At day's end, I turned off the electric typewriter, headed home to my wife and two kids for dinner and an evening of reading and TV. Forgotten were the pronouncements on the day's big issues since I doubted what I had to say would amount to much.

The Christmas Bureau editorial changed everything.

The voice again, the next morning. My tears had changed nothing. But the editorial struck a chord. At least that's what I concluded.

The voice went on and on about the truckloads of toys, canned goods and other gifts that had been delivered that day. This was the way I'd like to remember what the voice said. I suppose in reality only one or two pickup trucks dropped off the Christmas goodies. And the welcome delivery may well have come only as a coincidence to the appearance of my editorial.

In any case, I convinced myself that this Christmas story proved that editorials could make a difference. By golly, the do-gooder could sometimes do some good. I not only had a job. For me, I had a job even better than the ministry. I had a mission.

Chapter Nine

THE PERSONAL TOUCH

Your crusades to save the world usually don't start with Captain Ahab-like obsessions. Writing daily editorials under deadline is too much a seat-of-the-pants deal for the writer to think far ahead. Today's news story that has you so worked up over some injustice could very well be history by the time tomorrow's editions hit the street.

Moreover, something I figured out in the middle of my career: Writing on a topic week after week might keep the issue on the public agenda. Which would be a good start. But as a rule, editorials themselves don't move people to make big-time changes or end some injustice.

That discovery explains why I found myself, more and more, stepping out of the ivory tower of my Main Street office. As I grew bolder through the years, I would talk with public officials about the arguments I had raised in editorials. Often, I'd give them the telephone numbers of experts to contact.

I wrote a number of editorials calling for a ban on smoking in restaurants. But I also spoke to city council members about researchers who'd found a ban on smoking wouldn't hurt revenues. I wrote editorials deploring the way the police often handled the mentally ill, "mentals," the cops called them.

But I also sat in the mayor's office and urged him to adopt a Crisis Intervention Team, modeled after the Memphis Police Department, which had developed a national model for responding to citizens in psychosis.

I told school officials about experts they should invite to the city, and often that happened.

You'll see in my stories the dynamics of local politics, the grassroots of reform. It's something you won't find in a political science textbook. Each account features the struggle for justice of ordinary people against the powers that be or, just as often, against those who cling to the status quo.

Finally, while I consider these crusades at root to be reformist, conservatives joined them. Local issues aren't easily pigeonholed liberal or conservative. I would have enlisted anyone to a cause, without regard to their politics or ideology. Thoughtful people of every stripe can come together on things good for children, for clean air, for mental health.

The flip side of that axiom is that resistance to change can come from any position, too. Some liberals smoke. Some whack their kids. Some just love the status quo.

Those who resist can be powerful. Their desire to protect their turf can make them devious. Some who line up to block change will let you know you're not their friend. No surprise here, of course. As social reformer Saul Alinsky used to say, "Reform means movement, and movement means friction."

Sooner or later, you're going to make some people mad. That's the bargain the reformer makes. Stick to your principles, and you're going to piss off somebody.

Far more often, however, I found common cause with persons who had been on the other side. I was reminded again and again that no matter how much you believe in something, if you're going to enlist others to your cause, you've got to keep an open mind.

It often pays off big. After all, most people want to do the right thing. Granting them a respectful audience increases the chances they will.

In the first chapel service at Great Lakes, the Christian college I attended in Michigan, Jack Anderson, a South Carolina preacher in the area for evangelistic meetings, opened his sermon with this reminder:

"Students, there are a lot of good people in the world."

He spoke the sentence slowly, allowing the words to fill the room. Good people. The preacher's announcement has been my lodestar. It's profoundly influenced the way I see the world. I witness a cruelty. I hear of an injustice. And the preacher's words come back, and I know things can be OK. Jack Anderson's words, in his down-home, southern accent, remind me it is so.

No wonder, of the hundreds of chapel sermons I heard over eight years in religious schools, it's about the only thing from any sermon I remember.

Cynthia Valdizon

In my study at home, listening to a granddaughter

Chapter Ten

STORMING THE FORT

Fort Wayne can drive me nuts. It's the drivers who won't pull into the intersection to make a left turn. It's icy streets that make it scary to leave the house in the early morning to jog.

But it's not the conservatives. As a rule. Conservatives were among my faithful readers and my even more faithful critics.

If it weren't for them, I would have been preaching to the choir, a not uncommon exercise among pundits that hardly edifies the rest of the congregation. Naturally, I enjoyed hearing from the amen corner once in a while.

You take a liberal editorial page with conservative readers. If that paper's editorial writer hopes to change minds, he's got to be fair as an NFL referee and accurate as an atomic clock.

Conservative wears lots of faces. If you add "old-fashioned" to it, the idea refers to cautious, skeptical of change. My friend Will Clark says Fort Wayne is a "good enough" city. That nicely captures our community's caution.

In the 1940s, we chose not to have an interstate highway slicing through the downtown. In the 50s, we sat on our hands while outsiders schemed to create suburban shopping malls and doom downtown shopping.

In the 1960s we ducked the call of black leaders and white liberals to end segregation in the schools.

But for all this "good enough" stuff, along the way lots of good things cropped up. In fact, we're still a city inventing ourselves. Amoeba-like, we're forever changing form.

When people wanted a downtown convention center, those who objected didn't stop the project. They just took up a lot more time as we talked about it.

That happened with the art museum. Expansion of the

downtown library. And the dikes to prevent the three rivers the city straddles from destroying the houses built near a river. (I know, they shouldn't have been built there in the first place.)

Conservatives preach a doctrine that says "every man for himself." Just talk. When things get tough, conservatives will pull together just as quickly as liberals.

In 1982, as our heavy spring snows melted, the rivers overflowed big time. The flood nearly severed the north from the south side of the city. But our sandbaggers, kids, their parents, their grandparents turned out to create walls that held the rushing floodwaters at bay.

Our battle became a national news story. We were "the city that saved itself." My stay in Israel overlapped several days of the flood, and over state TV, I watched pictures of Fort Wayne's battle.

Conservatives joined with our moderates and liberals to rescue families whose breadwinner lost a union-wages job when our biggest private employer, International Harvester, pulled out. The company, with roots here that go back to the 1920s, got the brilliant idea to move operations to Springfield, Ohio.

Harvester bigwigs explained their Springfield buildings were more modern.

We said Harvester could go to Ohio and, while they were at it, they could go to hell for all we cared. To help the displaced workers, we raised money, set up food banks and offered loans so the displaced workers could get back on their feet.

Nevertheless, the loss of Harvester was a huge blow. Thousands of jobs, almost overnight, got swept away downstream like some debris left over from our floods.

Despite it all, city leaders scrambled to coax diverse companies to locate here. And what do you know? General Motors, the biggest manufacturer in the entire world, bought up a zillion acres of land just southwest of the city and plunked down a new truck plant.

We proved that when thousands of high-paying jobs are there for the asking, we suddenly put our conservative "good enough" habits aside and told a GM yes, yes, a thousand times, yes. We even shelled out millions of bucks in tax breaks just to show how much we love the corporation and the UAW, as well.

I didn't mention our religious conservatives? They settled this town just as much as the guys who steered the boats along the

Erie Canal, remnants of which can still be excavated here.

The city is home to the region's Catholic diocese, led by a Boston-bred Irishman. Missouri Synod Lutherans are a big presence. On the blocks the Catholics and Lutherans don't have a church, evangelicals have a building. The conservative groups have colleges here.

The towering spires belong mostly to the Catholics and Lutherans and the mainline Protestants like the Presbyterians and Methodists. Our more conservative churches can show lots of political clout.

That helps explain why the people we send to the General Assembly and to Congress are Republicans. Our few Democrats in office will tell you they're conservative. Especially on money matters, a point they open their speeches with.

We have about 100 black churches. Preachers and members vote Democratic but probably belong in the conservative column on theology and social issues.

If you're really looking for them, you can find liberals in social agencies, various churches, schools and at the regional campus of Indiana and Purdue Universities, now bursting at the seams with growth along the St. Joseph River on the north side. I've known a few liberal businessmen and women.

Four of our last five mayors have been fairly liberal, though I doubt they'd own up to it.

So, conservative by mood and slogans, we're a typical blue-collar town in the industrial Midwest. That mostly describes Indiana's population, from those who work in the aging steel mills of Gary to the shopkeepers in towns like Madison along the Ohio River.

Although we're Indiana's second-largest city, a big plus is that we act as if we're a small town. Everyone refers to city council members by their first names. If you hang around the courthouse, you hear the judges referred to by their first names—Charlie, Fran, John, Steve, Kenny and so forth. Everybody knows who you're talking about.

Our conservative reputation has spread far abroad. I once got an award for my editorials on religious freedom from the liberal People for the American Way. That's the group Norman Lear founded. At the ceremony in New York, the board chairman, former Rep. John Buchanan, made a big deal over how much courage I showed to write such liberal stuff in a conservative city.

Accepting the plaque, I confessed it didn't take all that much courage at all. Even vehement critics remained civil. The one threat of bodily harm I got in all my years at the paper came over an editorial about Oliver North's role in the Iran-contra scandal. I didn't even write the piece.

I found, rather, that if you don't make a big deal out of somebody's beliefs, conservative or liberal, you're apt to get a receptive audience. Just tell them your concerns and give them the facts. That's all you have to do.

As you'll see in my stories, this proved to be a good strategy. A few of this old liberal's crusades prevailed. Just when you think you've got it figured out, this conservative fort will fool you every time.

Chapter Eleven

DONNA'S FIRE

It just made me ill when I read the front page story over breakfast. The 14-year-old Huntington girl would be tried as an adult.

Now I concede that committing a major crime is a powerful way for a teenager to get people to pay attention: You set fire to the family home, as this girl did, kill your mother and sister, though you may not have meant to, and then pray like the devil nobody gets too mad at you.

It's not that simple, though. Not in America. Not in Indiana. And for goodness sakes not in Huntington, Indiana, home of former Vice President Dan Quayle. This is a town where family values to some people mean you do what your mother tells you, even if she occasionally beats the crap out of you.

Out here in the heartland, we can let our horror over some violent crime a kid commits get the better of us. That's understandable. We read in the paper that on a drizzly night after a big family row a girl does something really scary. It makes us wonder what the kids we know right next door might be up to some day. We're not sure we want to know more of the girl's story. To our great loss, in my opinion.

My first editorial about Donna Ratliff asked, "Why did Donna kill her mother?"

Over the weeks after the fire, I collected stacks of reports about the abuse in the Ratliff family. I listened to eyewitness accounts of the aftermath of the fire. Suffice it that Donna had her reasons, as nutty as they were, for setting that fire back in 1995.

The Ratliff family screw-ups in the child-rearing department shouldn't have been a mystery to the Huntington prosecutor or to the Circuit Court judge.

Even if I hadn't heard of the abuse, I thought it was crazy to treat this troubled kid as some hardened adult criminal. But the prosecutor and the judge didn't seem to know that putting violent young offenders in the adult system made the kids more likely to commit crimes when they got out.

In their defense, Huntington officials were in the majority of Americans on the subject of how to treat violent young offenders.

Prosecuting a kid as an adult, you've basically given up on rehabilitation and say it's OK to administer vengeance and hope the kid isn't more of a mess when he or she eventually gets out of prison.

But if you give a second thought to housing kids with tough adult criminals, which almost nobody does, you'd realize it was a pretty stupid idea, although most states, including Indiana, have been doing it for years.

How a kid can make sense of an adult criminal trial, and have the slightest idea of what it would mean to be locked up for years on end, well, that remains a mystery to me.

I first met Donna at the Huntington County Jail. It was in August, three months after the fire.

She didn't look me in the eye much. If I hadn't known she was 14, I would have taken her for a younger child. She wore a grey sweatshirt. Her straight brown hair fell over her forehead and draped over her shoulders, as if to conceal as much of her face as possible.

Her blue eyes really stood out, a deeper shade of blue than most. If you didn't know better, you might have guessed she was wearing those tinted contact lenses. Also, you couldn't miss that this was one mad-as-hell kid.

Once she started talking, her litany of complaints poured out by the bushels.

Her mother had beaten the girl. She wouldn't let her visit her father during his second-shift break at the factory. And her mother played favorites. Donna claimed the oldest sister, at the time of the fire living with a grandmother in Kentucky, had been her mother's love child. As far as Donna was concerned, it all damned her mother.

What about the happy memories of her mother? Surely, she had some, I suggested.

My question got her to change tone and, briefly, a Shirley Temple lilt took over her voice. (You could see why people had Donna pegged as a master manipulator.) Yes, she explained, the family had taken this trip to the Indiana Dunes, a popular resort in northwest Indiana.

Then, in the next breath, she returned to her disjointed bitching about her mom. None of it, of course, meant her mother Glissie deserved the death penalty. Donna only briefly mentioned Jamie, the sister who also died in the fire.

After an hour visiting the girl, I found myself depressed. I wondered whether any amount of counseling could undo the damage done to this child.

I was clear about one thing. I saw little hope for Donna's redemption in an adult prison. I walked out into the sunshine in silence, not bothering to say goodbye to Sheriff Rod Jackson.

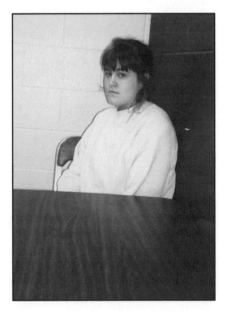

Courtesy the Journal Gazette

Donna in our first meeting

Chapter Twelve

GLISSIE AND JAMIE

"Mom's still a big problem, just not as bad," Jamie Ratliff wrote to her older sister Tammy in Kentucky two years before the fire that claimed her life.

I caught hell in Huntington for writing a lot of editorials about Donna Ratliff and not saying much about the victims of the fire, Donna's mother Glissie and her 16-year-old sister, Jamie.

Well, looking back, I can see I deserved some criticism. I guess most everybody involved in the case, and those who followed it, ignored Glissie and Jamie. I don't count my viewing the video of the autopsies, which I did out of idle curiosity.

When they were mentioned in court, it often came across as vague and incomplete. They might just as well have been identified as prosecutor's Exhibits A and B.

No victim's rights group stepped forward to demand a fitting memorial in front of the charred frame house on Grayston Street. (When I visited the remodeled house a year later, Perry, Donna's father, still kept the picture of his wife in a downstairs closet.)

No plaque honoring Jamie materialized on the wall at the high school. (At many schools, if you're a football star killed in a car accident or if you're a soldier and enemy fire takes your life, you get a plaque.)

"Who speaks for the two people who died in that fire?" Judge McIntosh asked, to no one in particular when he was sentencing 14-year-old Donna. Around the courtroom, people nodded their heads. But nobody stood to interrupt and speak for Glissie and Jamie.

Glissie remains the most puzzling of the characters in the Ratliff case. (I never got to know the eldest Ratliff daughter, Tammy, a college student, who lived with her grandmother in Kentucky at the time of the fire.)

When I visited the Grayston Avenue house after it had been

repaired, a shelf with a group of ceramic figurines caught my eye. It was Glissie's collection, English lords and ladies in various poses. Somebody had cleaned the soot from the fire off them. Perry had arranged them as best he could remember where his wife had placed them.

Calm and order prevail among the fragile figures. The collection gives you a glimpse into this woman's heart. She valued pretty things. She liked to show them off.

Donna had mentioned the figurines as her mother's most prized possession. That's why the girl, in her rage toward her mother, doused them with kerosene just before torching the family home. The smoke had turned them black but didn't destroy them.

The figurines gave you one side of Glissie. Then you had this other side. She abused her girls. This she freely admitted to counselors. She hit them in the face with her open hand and with her fists. Once, a classmate of Jamie's walked into the house unannounced for a visit only to discover Glissie on top of Donna, beating the girl.

One counselor's report mentioned that Glissie beat the girls with a belt when they were slow getting up for school. Volunteers at the Salvation Army's Teen Center saw marks on Donna's leg they judged to have been made by a broom handle.

The girls knew only too well their mother's wrath. Capt. Ken Nicolai, the Salvation Army minister, one of Donna's defenders, found Jamie and Donna at a railroad underpass one evening. Both were sobbing. They feared going home until their father got off work later that night.

Did Glissie put the girls out for prostitution, as Donna claimed? The investigator for Donna's attorney found two men at a bar in nearby North Manchester who claimed it was so. Yet that always seemed out of character for what I knew of Glissie. The physical abuse was another matter.

The beatings of Donna had a history. One of the girl's elementary school teachers told me how the girl often came to school with scratches and bruises on her arms, which she explained was the result of getting into a fight with another kid. The teacher guessed somebody at home had inflicted the injuries. Students who had been at the middle school Donna attended told me they often saw Donna crying, trembling at her desk or by herself on the playground.

The reports of social workers and counselors further

described the Ratliff household as one where angry words and threats of severe punishment filled the air. You could say the family climate itself amounted to abuse.

Thus, the stage was set for tragedy. Long before the fire, the girls tried to deal with the abuse. Reading reports and talking to people in Huntington, I kept coming across accounts of the girls running away from home. (Donna, seemingly, couldn't remember how often.) She once got all the way on a Greyhound bus from northern Indiana to Nashville, Tennessee.

Not a happy home.

I suppose it was the stories of abuse that stirred me and others as much as her age.

But just as kids aren't born to set fire to the family home and kill their mothers and sisters, mothers aren't born to beat their kids with belt buckles and flip-flops, another of Glissie's weapons. Records of counseling centers and social workers matter-of-factly reported that both Glissie and Perry's parents had abused them.

I shared all this with New York Times reporter Fox Butterfield, who wrote a front page article on the case, attracting national attention. Butterfield heard a few things I hadn't. In a phone interview, Perry Ratliff told him that the first time he had sex with Glissie—she would have been 14—she said it reminded her of the way her father did it.

I doubt Glissie ever mentioned such things to her daughters. To counselors, she only talked of her own abuse in the most general terms. She carried the knowledge of how many times her own father sexually molested her to the grave.

No wonder that when she was merely 15 she ran off with Perry to West Virginia to get married.

Still, now I look at pictures Donna sent me of her mother, and I have trouble understanding how such an attractive, seemingly happy woman could feel such anger toward her own kids. In one photograph, seven-year-old Donna sits on her mother's lap, and Santa Claus seems to be balancing both of them on his knee.

Dark brown hair, sparkling hazel eyes, Glissie holds Donna with both hands around the child's chest and smiles back at the camera. What a pleasant, likable person, I say to myself every time I glance at the photograph.

Glissie endeared herself to the people outside the home, such as those at the fundamentalist church she attended and the women she worked the hard hours with at Eagle-Picher Plastics in

Huntington. One co-worker, Amanda Voirol, told me she thinks of Glissie every day.

"She was such a wonderful person."

"All she cared about was her girls and seeing that they got a college education."

Yet one time, Voirol got a glimpse of dark cloud that hung over the Ratliff family.

During their break, just days before the fire, she found Glissie crying at her work station.

"What's the matter, Glissie?"

"Donna says she's going to kill me."

Whose heart wouldn't go out to a mother so vexed and troubled?

But a full account of Glissie must also look at the face her daughters saw so often.

"A hard woman." That was how juvenile probation officer Gwen Bechtol described Glissie.

"She just didn't know how to discipline her girls."

It's an observation that echoes again and again in court records.

Nevertheless, counselors and social workers found Glissie willing to give it a try, evidence of the truth of the co-worker's observation. Meantime, Perry, the permissive father, undercut her efforts at every turn, letting the kids smoke and stay out late. Once, Glissie entered into a contract with a counselor. She signed a promise to stop beating the kids.

Days later, after the girls had disobeyed her, she declared, "The contract is off." One can only conclude the beatings resumed.

For all the disappointments, the false starts and the counseling sessions, Glissie never gave up. Even on the night of the fire, she summoned Nanda Wilson, the social worker, to the home during a fight with Donna. I can't imagine many families that reached out for help so often or many other mothers who were so determined to keep rebellious teenagers in the household.

Wilson had visited the home 55 times before the fire. After one big fight with Donna, she asked Glissie if it wasn't time to remove the girls from the home. (The welfare department had placed Donna in foster care twice, though only for a few days.)

"No, I can handle it," Glissie replied, to tragic consequences for herself and her daughter Jamie. I read the transcript of that fateful conversation several times to be sure I read it right.

For me, however, nothing compares to an insight into the family like Jamie's letter to her sister Tammy.

If Jamie, soon to be a junior, didn't stand out at Huntington North High School, people liked her. Donna would put tacks on the sidewalks for kids to run over with their bicycles. Jamie played with the neighbor kids.

In parts of her letter, she sounds like the most happy-go-lucky kid in the world. She tells her distant sister of her plans to swim and bike every day that summer to get a tan. She boasts how she can make people laugh in person but not so well in writing.

She shares teenage gossip with Tammy about who's dating whom and how she's soon to break up with Shawn because she would have cheated on him. The style of the letter is mostly breezy. You can see how those who knew her described her in positive terms.

Indeed, calmer, more mature than Donna, Jamie got along well with her teachers. Her school pictures show her to be pretty, though not exceptionally so. (In the letter, she jokes about being overweight: "1,000 lbs. NOT, only 135.")

I admire how Jamie could laugh at herself. I never saw that trait in Donna.

Perry told me that Donna couldn't get enough attention from him, although Jamie could be independent. But when Jamie was only 14, she worried that a family tragedy lay ahead.

I found the letter particularly poignant when Jamie asks the older sister if she can ever remember her mother having fun with them as a family. She can't, she says. Yet their dad is almost always happy, she continues. Her mother, however, seems forever complaining, about money, about the house not being clean.

"Dad only complains when Mom is on his back," Jamie adds parenthetically.

She loves her dad more than her mom. She says that straight out.

From that admission, Jamie goes on to say she's glad the sister is trying to heal some wounds, a reference to whatever unhappy events that led the parents to send Tammy to her grandmother's to finish school in Kentucky.

"Tammy, sometimes I'm scared of Donna," Jamie says as the letter takes on an ominous tone.

"After I tell you this, you'd get scared, too."

Jamie's story is of Donna's suicide attempts, first with pills, then with a knife. Jamie mentions the date, April 1, 1993.

"I stopped her but the knife cut me."

"I'm still afraid she will kill me and her. Because we're not getting along."

At the time the house fire claimed her life, Jamie had been on probation. Glissie had her arrested for stealing her ATM card—somehow the girl knew the PIN number—and withdrawing money to give to her friends so they could buy beer.

Nevertheless, the probation officer's last report on Jamie glowed. She had a job at McDonald's so she could pay her mother back. Her grades at school were picking up. She talked of someday becoming a teacher.

Prosecutor John Branham said he didn't believe Donna meant to kill Jamie in the fire, just their mother.

In the quiet of a Huntington cemetery, two gravestones, side by side, mark the final resting place of Glissie and Jamie Ratliff. Their rightful legacy is to be remembered.

Ratliff Family album

The kinder, gentler Glissie and Donna

Chapter Thirteen

HER JUDGE

Here's this 14-year-old child walking into the Huntington circuit courtroom, escorted by Sheriff Jackson, dragging a sadness like a sack of potatoes, all dolled up in a black jumper with white blouse, dark brown hair pulled back, nodding slightly toward her friends who had come for the occasion.

I watch her and think if not for the circumstances, a criminal proceeding, you might mistake this girl for a receptionist in a realty office. She is a killer, though.

It's December. This is northern Indiana so of course it's cold. I'm eager to get to the courtroom, eager to learn Donna Ratliff's fate. I take two steps at a time up to the courthouse door. Snowflakes swirl around my head, and I'm quickly in the old building's stifling warmth.

I'm early, and peek into the courtroom. It's a solemn room with blue and gold designs on the walls framed in marble. Tables for the defense and prosecution match the colors of the walls. (Surely, no judge chose the decor.)

Too high on the wall to be much noticed hang portraits of Thomas Jefferson, John Marshall and Samuel Huntington, a signer of the Declaration of Independence after whom the town is named. The trio appears corpse-like, indifferent to daily proceedings, from child custody hearings to murder trials. I scribble in my notebook.

Donna's supporters, sporting baby-blue ribbons, have taken seats on the left side, behind the defense counsel's table. No trial by jury this day. The girl had pleaded guilty to arson and reckless homicide. This was public record. Nevertheless, there would be testimony. Mostly, we were there to hear the sentence. It's too late for the judge to look at the girl, take note of how young she is and say he made a mistake in transferring her to the criminal court.

At that moment, she can't buy cigarettes, drive or vote. But she's going to get an adult sentence and, likely, will be sent to an adult prison.

Before the proceedings get underway, I hang out in the hallway, on the third floor. People talk quietly as if during a calling at the funeral home down on East Washington Street.

The buzz among reporters and onlookers concerns the inflammatory remarks Perry Ratliff had just made before television cameras.

"If she comes after anyone else in the family, I'll take her out." The bluster was right in character. Perry loves an audience.

Back in the courtroom, on schedule, Huntington Circuit Judge Mark McIntosh enters from the right. We all stand as the judge takes his seat, the bench elevated only a few inches above the main floor. This truly is the people's court. The first time I met Judge McIntosh he teased me about telling him what to do, referring to my editorials. I, mindful my daily editorials advised nearly everyone what to do, told him he'd have to take his place in line to complain.

Outgoing and personable, McIntosh is in his mid-60s, a full head of greying hair, not tall, stockily built as befitting the Michigan State football player he once was. In his chambers, he'll show you pictures of the courthouse in its sundry incarnations through the years. (Once a high school history teacher, he is the acknowledged historian of the building and glows with pride as he points out its marvels to a visitor.) On this day, he had a young girl on his mind and the two people in her family that she had killed.

I find my way to the row of seats reserved for the media, just off to the side of the judge's bench. I squeeze into a seat between reporters, one a kid from the high school paper, the other for the Huntington Herald Press, whose otherwise congenial editor said he had no sympathy for Donna Ratliff.

Surveying the courtroom, I have the impression almost everybody was on the verge of tears. Filling seats on the right, sitting behind the prosecutor, is the family of Donna's mother, plainly distressed and grieving over their losses anew. On the other side the girl's supporters look grim, fearing a harsh sentence yet hoping the judge could find a way to salvage Donna's life.

I had been writing about the case from the beginning. At first, I complained about the transfer of a young juvenile to the adult criminal court. It had happened nevertheless. As I dug deeper into the case, I learned of a new state law concerning such kids and urged the judge to invoke it. The law, sponsored by state

Rep. Dennis Avery of Evansville, fit Donna Ratliff's situation perfectly.

It allowed a judge to recommend that the Department of Correction place such a young offender in a private, secure treatment center for juveniles. Otherwise, in Indiana at the time, and in most other states, such a girl would be sent to an adult prison where she would receive little if any psychological treatment and no proper schooling.

Moreover, in an adult prison, I argued often, she would associate with hardened adult offenders, the worst kind of role models for a teenager.

I couldn't tell from my earlier conversations in his chambers whether the judge had bought my argument. (As a rule, judges won't tip their hand to a journalist, even on an "off the record" basis.) Now, at the hearing, I would know McIntosh's decision soon enough.

From the defense table, Donna answers his questions, whether she understands the charges against her, whether she understands the plea bargain and whether she was in agreement.

"Yes, yes, yes," come her replies, barely audible.

Shortly after, veteran Huntington Prosecutor John Branham stands to lay out the case. Middle-aged, with greying temples, he speaks with a nasal tone and often without facial expression, implying a seriousness he may not always intend.

Indeed, from his grave, almost angry demeanor, you might guess he is trying a pair of murderous bank robbers, not helping the judge determine the sentence for a screwed-up 14-year-old.

Nevertheless, Branham had sensibly agreed to reduce the murder charge to reckless homicide. That greatly cuts the number of years she would be locked up. The arson charge stands. Right now, he speaks movingly of Glissie and Jamie who had lost their lives. To his credit, he does not oppose a juvenile placement for the girl.

I jot in my notebook that Donna's court-appointed attorney, Stephen Michael, does a good job of showing just how profoundly troubled the Ratliff family had been, focusing on the abuse that set the stage for the girl's rash act. Like the prosecutor, Michael is middle-aged, serious and yet also carries a weariness about him I've noticed in other veteran defense attorneys.

It's left to the investigator for the defense, Cheri Guavera from Indianapolis, to lay out the details of the dysfunction in the family. Her extensive interviews with neighbors, friends and fellow workers reveal a shocking family history in which normal expressions of love get lost amid the screaming matches, threats of violence and beatings. (Court documents from social agencies and police back up this sad portrait.)

We haven't heard the last of Perry Ratliff. He's hired his own attorney, which only served to raise suspicions anew about his role in this tragedy. Called to the stand, he strides forward like a graduate marching toward the platform for his diploma.

This day, dressed in a black and grey fatigue shirt, he wears his hair slicked down with bangs over his forehead. He pleads with the judge to impose the maximum penalty on his daughter.

I often said Perry could have come right out of Dogpatch, Al Capp's hillbilly village of the "Little Abner" comic strip. In fact, Perry did grow up in poverty in Kentucky. He once told me that all of his brothers and sisters, except for one sister, had been in trouble with the law. Their father, an alcoholic who sold the family's food to buy liquor, regularly had beaten them.

Years later, married, with three daughters, Perry had disengaged from the raising of the girls. The counselors all made that point. He had left that to the emotionally fragile Glissie.

Months after this hearing, over fried chicken at Penguin Point, he recalled to me how they had been separated six times and divorced once. At the time of the fire, and for some months before, he had been sleeping on the couch downstairs, not with his wife.

Now, blustering on the stand in the Huntington courtroom, he wants the judge to see color photographs he had taken of Glissie's head at the funeral home. Perry, it seems, is on a roll this day. The photos, he explains, show bruises under the hair that had been combed down.

Perry contends that Donna had hit her mother with a hammer before she set the fire. That would have made the crime seem even worse, calling for more severe punishment.

Eyeing the man over horn-rimmed glasses, the judge brushes aside Perry's testimony, and almost in an aside, he says the marks had not been injurious. (I told the Fort Wayne pathologist about the exchange. He took exception to the judge's remark, noting he had also found suspicious marks on Glissie's neck, although she and Jamie both died of smoke inhalation.)

Indianapolis psychologist Robert Ten Eych is called to the stand. In his examination of Donna, one of many conducted of the girl, he concludes, "You find in Donna the things you usually find in an abused child."

He goes on to argue that without extensive therapy, Donna's problems could worsen and, later in life, her conduct disorder might well develop into an antisocial personality. Ten Eych, whose testimony the judge warmly commends, urges that Donna be placed in a good juvenile center. I knew of one such place for sure.

Weeks before the hearing, I had contacted John Link, head of psychological services at Crossroad Children's Home in Fort Wayne. Link and one of his counselors interviewed Donna twice at the county jail and thought prospects for successful treatment at the private center were good. In court, Link tells the judge Crossroad had a secure unit and would accept Donna, offering her treatment and schooling.

So what was McIntosh going to make of it all? Unfurling a sheaf of yellow legal-size papers, he begins quoting from social agency reports about the family. Although he doubts some of Donna's claims of abuse—I assume that included her lurid story that her mother had prostituted her and Jamie—he concedes much abuse occurred. No, that doesn't excuse Donna, he emphasizes. Nonetheless, looking directly at her, he says, "There were more than two victims to the tragic fire," plainly referring to Donna.

As an aside, McIntosh chastises the agencies and police for not sharing what they knew about the family's problems. The failure to share, he finds, "heartbreaking." It was a criticism of the agencies Huntington welfare director Ron Mitchell later said "came out of left field."

What of the family members, I wonder. For McIntosh, they seem to be in "complete denial" about the impact of the abuse on Donna. Counselors, he thinks, blamed the family's problems on the girl. Summing up the record, he goes on, "We have all failed Donna." Then, preparing to announce the sentence, he asks, with some emotion, "Who speaks for Glissie and Jamie from the grave?"

Despite the evidence of the abuse Donna struggled with, he can only conclude the heinousness of the crime cancels out such mitigating factors. Shifting to a matter-of-fact tone, the judge imposes a sentence of 25 years, 15 for the arson, five years for each death. Given the length of the sentence, I'm not expecting what follows.

Going on, McIntosh announces he's forwarding to the Department of Correction a list of juvenile treatment centers, including Crossroad in Fort Wayne. Now that's the kind of place Donna belongs, I think, nodding toward the reporter sitting next to me. Indeed, a juvenile center is what the judge "sincerely" recommends.

"Yes!" I declare to myself, clinching my fist and punching the air in victory. Shortly afterward, I discover it's only halftime. This game ain't over.

Larry Hayes

In chambers, Judge McIntosh shows me his family

Chapter Fourteen

NO PLACE FOR KIDS

Naturally they sent her to prison.

I had a pretty good idea of why Commissioner Chris DeBruyn refused to follow Judge McIntosh's advice to the Department of Correction to place Donna Ratliff in a private juvenile center.

It was partly money. A center like Crossroad sends the state of Indiana a bill of $80,000 a year to house a kid in a locked unit. Donna's keep at the Women's Prison in Indianapolis would cost $20,000.

DeBruyn could see where all this could be going. What if the Huntington judge's recommendation gave other judges in the state's 92 counties the notion of how to handle a disturbed kid who had committed a terrible crime?

That would run up a bill no DOC commissioner would care to get.

And what's he supposed to do with the 100 or so other kids under 18 already in state adult prisons? If he moves one girl, how could he justify not moving others, with an equally troubled past?

Moreover, moving the Ratliff girl to a private treatment center wasn't likely to show that the state was getting tough on juvenile crime. Unfortunately, that's what policymakers think the public demands.

During the debate on the Ratliff case, I often heard the phrase, "Do the crime, you do the time."

But if they wanted, state leaders and judges easily could have checked out the research on the transfer of juveniles. In Indiana and most other states, these kids would end up in an adult prison.

In his 2003 landmark book, *Preventing & Reducing Juvenile Delinquency,* James "Buddy" Howell notes that nearly all of 50 studies have found one overriding fact: Kids transferred to the criminal courts are more likely than those retained in the juvenile system to repeat a crime after they're released.

Throughout the Ratliff saga, I consulted Buddy more often than any expert. He's the former head of research for the U.S. Office of Juvenile Justice and Delinquency Prevention and a crackerjack of a scholar.

Over the phone, in his friendly, Texas-bred accent, he would point out that the repeat offenses not only are higher among the kids transferred to the criminal courts. They were more likely to commit a crime more quickly and commit a more serious offense. (It's also true that kids in prison are more likely than adults to be assaulted or raped.)

You might assume juveniles who are transferred to criminal court had committed terrible crimes. In Indiana, that applies to only half of the young offenders. That's true elsewhere, as well. The rest of these kids simply managed to piss off adults with minor offenses enough times for a judge to decide the juvenile system couldn't rehabilitate them.

I imagine that in their hearts, judges understand that to transfer a juvenile offender to the adult court is to write off the kid. After all, in this day and age, prisons are meant to punish, not rehabilitate. That's a given.

But the judges also are responding to something else here. That's the anguish survivors of a juvenile crime suffer day after day. It is an anguish that often expresses itself in a blind rage toward a violent young juvenile. How could a judge with any human feeling not try to assuage those feelings among family members? It factors in the calculus.

I saw this in the Ratliff case and in others as well. Indeed, I often found myself wanting to console these people.

In Antwerp, Ohio, a small town east of Fort Wayne just across the state line, a teenager named Mindy Berynl waited for her abusive father to come home from work one afternoon. Then she shot him to death with his own shotgun. This was just a few months after the Huntington fire. (Counselors had warned him the girl had threatened to kill her dad.)

I wrote an editorial or two about the case. I simply urged the county judge in Ohio not to transfer Mindy to the criminal court. Like Donna Ratliff, this girl had a history of serious emotional problems. She belonged in a juvenile center for treatment, not packed off to the state prison.

Family members were furious with me. They couldn't have been angrier if I had applauded Mindy for knocking off her old man.

In a Fort Wayne case, an African-American boy, 12-year-old Jamone Williams, was charged with shooting to death an older gentleman, Prince Chapman. One account likely explained the motive, such as it was: The man had scolded the boy one night in front of his friends as they hung around a street corner. Jamone blasted the man.

As if to make the crime seem even more inexcusable, Chapman was well known as an advocate for the same kind of kids. I had known Prince and his commitment to these kids. I guessed he would have been the first to oppose transferring the boy to the criminal court.

To be sure, this kid was bad news. At age 12, the boy and his twin brother already had compiled a juvenile record for armed robbery. (It remained a mystery to me why some adult wasn't locked up for letting a 12-year-old acquire a handgun.)

My editorials opposed the transfer. I invoked the same arguments I had in the Ratliff case. And provoked the same wrath from the victim's family that my writing had provoked in the Ohio case.

Early on, I called Prince's widow. I hoped she might also oppose the transfer. But she just repeated her demand the boy be severely punished.

So I had to pin my hopes that the juvenile court judge, Steve Sims, a former county prosecutor, would reject the transfer. I helped the boy's defense attorney, also a former prosecutor, connect with a nationally respected Indiana University child psychiatrist, Dr. Ted Petti.

Ted examined the boy at length. Then, in a hearing on the transfer, he told the judge it would be a "disaster" to put this child in the adult system. The boy not only was too young to participate meaningfully in a criminal proceeding. He had an IQ low enough to qualify him as a special education student. Moreover, his severe diabetes made him prone to irrational outbursts. On top of it all, many of Jamone's family members were or had been in prison.

This kid's story cried out for extensive treatment.

Unfortunately, the prosecutor called a local psychiatrist and local psychologist to testify. Even though neither specialized in children and adolescents, and neither enjoys a reputation as a forensic expert, they recommended the transfer.

After his testimony, I chatted with the local psychiatrist in the hall. He told me that for him and his colleague, "It came down to a toss of the coin." A few days later, the judge announced his ruling. To my dismay, he ignored Dr. Petti's authoritative testimony and deferred to the local guys. I think he saw the boy as a lost cause. Even the defense attorney told me later that if he had been the judge, he would have transferred the boy, too.

But the Ratliff case taught me one thing. Once you can get the person to separate the issue of housing a serious juvenile offender from the issue of punishment, your chances of winning him or her over dramatically improve.

In the year following the Ratliff fire in Huntington, I joined colleagues on the editorial page to interview candidates for the Indiana General Assembly. An editorial board draws on such interviews to help decide the paper's endorsements for the election. Because The Journal Gazette circulates throughout the region, we interviewed a lot of candidates for every election. Those who showed up were a motley crew. We unearthed moderate Republicans. We met right-wing Democrats.

Because I had become so obsessed with the issue, I always inquired of the candidate what his or her view was on housing kids in prison with adults. I made a point of saying that the juvenile would still serve the sentence and thereby would "pay for his or her crime."

I left the whole question of transfers to another day. But if I stuck to the question of how to house the kids, I found even the most conservative candidate could agree it's only smart to put kids in juvenile centers, separate from hardened adult criminals.

In these discussions, I often whipped out a quote from one of the framers of the Indiana Constitution, back in 1850.

Delegates to that long-ago gathering were debating amendments to the newly adopted constitution. Kids in prisons came up. Delegates wanted language to require the state to provide "houses of refuge" for juvenile offenders.

A Mr. Bryant of Warren, a town just south of Fort Wayne, cited one case in which the state had placed brothers, one 14, the other only 10, in the state prison. He demanded to know:

"How do you propose to diminish crime or to reform offenders by this system of sending the children of the state, perhaps the victims of dissolute parents and neglected education, to this school of vice and infamy, where they cannot fail by means of the associations into which you thrust them, to be irretrievably ruined?"

Good old Mr. Bryant of Warren. That was my gospel.

Meantime, I went to lawmakers from the Fort Wayne area to see if they would introduce bills in Indiana House and Senate that would require the physical separation of the juveniles from adults.

Indeed, bills were introduced. I went to the statehouse to hear Republican state Sen. Bud Meeks, a former county sheriff, argue before one committee in the Senate chamber for the separation. He was downright passionate about it.

Democratic state Rep. Ben GiaQuinta helped draft another bill in the House. Ben asked me to write up a talking paper for him, which he then used in a hearing before a House committee.

Democratic state Rep. Win Moses, a former Fort Wayne mayor, joined GiaQuinta. The bill came within a heartbeat of becoming law. But it got lost in a partisan wrangle that had nothing to do with young offenders.

Another Republican senator, Tom Wyss, proposed a blue-ribbon commission to take up the issue. A few years later, the governor did sign legislation to create such a commission. At this writing, the commission continues to conduct hearings on revisions to the juvenile code.

So while Judge McIntosh didn't see his recommendation followed right away, major changes in the treatment of young offenders were in the works. As the publicity on the Ratliff case heated up, thanks in no small part to The New York Times story, even the Department of Correction responded.

Not long after she was sent there, the women's prison, in the seedy, working class neighborhood of eastern Indianapolis, created a youthful offender unit. Officials promised special programs that would help those kids succeed in the outside world.

A few years later, the DOC created youthful offender units at two of the prisons for men.

I'm afraid we're a long way off from eliminating transfers. I grant that a few young offenders may have been so damaged they're beyond recovery. Others are so close to age 18 that the courts are likely to look upon them as adults.

But for the young kids like Donna Ratliff and Jamone Williams, just maybe we've seen progress. The transfers have dropped. Since the Ratliff girl was first sent to the women's prison, the number of kids in adult prisons has fallen from 100 to 60. That's good, for two reasons. First, keeping kids in the juvenile system improves the chances the kid will be rehabilitated. Second, it promotes the public safety.

I'd be kidding myself if I thought judges had seen the light. No doubt, part of the drop reflects the decline in juvenile crime the entire country has seen since the early 1990s. But I bet part of the change says a few judges are more reluctant to agree to the transfers. They're problematic for yet another reason.

A 2003 study of 1,400 young people from 11 to 24 by Lawrence Steinberg and his researchers at Temple University showed how the transfers could be cut even further.

The Temple study found that a third of children 11 through 13 and one-fifth of those 14 or 15 had a terribly limited grasp of legal matters. In fact, these kids' competence amounted to no better an understanding of court proceedings than that of mentally ill adults who are found incompetent to stand trial.

Not only are the younger kids less able to follow court proceedings, those with lower intelligence, such as Jamone Williams, are even more unlikely to figure out what's going on.

To be sure, most courts order psychological testing for a juvenile up for a transfer. But currently available testing doesn't probe the juvenile's grasp of the simple issues an adult would be expected to understand.

That's a tricky matter. The latest research shows that the juvenile's brain isn't fully developed. So when a Donna Ratliff tells the judge she understands a plea bargain, her answer, which she's been coached to give, doesn't necessarily mean she does.

As this research filters into the criminal justice system, and particularly as defense attorneys become aware of it, I believe we'll see judges asking for the sort of reliable tests, not currently available, that can determine whether a juvenile can follow criminal proceedings in a meaningful fashion and aid in his or her defense.

(In the Ratliff case, Dr. Ten Eych declared that Donna was competent in a legal sense. But as I looked at the tests he administered, I saw none that probed her grasp of the law.)

More than 230,000 kids are transferred to criminal courts each year. That's a lot of kids to write off. It's a lot of kids that could be exposed to the abuse of an adult prison. It's a lot of kids to turn over to an institution that doesn't really protect the public—no matter what the age of the offender.

Most of all, these transfers represent an admission of failure, offering neither the education nor the therapy so young offenders have a shot to become decent citizens. It's something I wish every editorial writer and every child advocate would harp on until it's fixed.

Chapter Fifteen

JAILBIRD

"My God, she's young."

Superintendent Dana Blank's eyes widened and she jerked her head back when I showed her a recent photograph of Donna Ratliff. I was visiting the prison just a couple of weeks after she was sentenced.

Blank reminded me of Mrs. Pyncheon, the regal, no-nonsense newspaper publisher in the old "Lou Grant" TV series.

I thought to myself, "Well what do you expect a 14-year-old girl to look like?" But I kept my mouth shut and didn't say that the state had no business putting this immature, very troubled kid in the Indiana Women's Prison. After all this is where the state sent its worst female offenders.

Donna's age qualified her as the youngest inmate in the 100-year history of the place. That is, if the Department of Correction refused to follow Judge McIntosh's recommendation.

Before I met Superintendent Blank in her office, Gary Scott, her assistant, showed me around. He gave me a bit of the background on the prison, told me how more than 90 percent of its inmates—his guesstimate—had been sexually molested. He said most of the women, about 400, had been convicted of drug and related offenses—casualties in the War on Drugs.

The prison projects the aesthetics of a waterfront warehouse. It covers a couple of blocks along busy New York Street on the poorer east side of Indianapolis. You'd need to be a high school pole-vaulter to get over the 12-foot chain-link fence. Even then the razor wire on top of the fence could rip a person up pretty bad making the bid to escape.

As I looked around at the scattering of red-brick buildings, I could believe it's just what's advertised. The facades needed attention, some cleaning up, years ago. To get in to visit an inmate, you're checked through several gates. Litter from the busy street piles up daily outside the fence. The somber, African-American guard at the front gate will tell you to take the two-inch Swiss Army knife on your key chain back to your car. Is it possible to segregate Donna from the older prisoners? No, Scott tells me. She will have to mix with the general population, average age 26. Schooling? Well, she could take a sewing class. She'd get to prepare for the GED. (Too bad, at 14, she wasn't old enough to take the test to get the GED certificate.)

As for high school, let it be known that the Indiana Women's Prison does not offer high school courses. You could sign up for them at Girls' School also in Indianapolis, if a juvenile judge sent you there. Oh yes, in a few years, after Donna earned the GED, she could enroll in college courses that Ball State professors who drive down from Muncie offer in the evenings.

I was disappointed to learn how little the prison could do to accommodate the young girl. Nevertheless, Blank promised to do all she could to help straighten the girl out. She went on, assuring me that she'd give Donna "a lot of mothering." I'm sure Blank didn't appreciate the grim irony in her vow.

The Huntington sheriff took Donna to Indianapolis and the prison. This stop was to be only for intake and would last a few weeks. After that, I assumed DOC Commissioner Chris DeBruyn would honor the judge's request and ship the girl back up north, very likely to the juvenile treatment center in Fort Wayne. Boy was I naive.

When will DeBruyn move Donna? I asked his spokeswoman, Pam Pattison.

"She has been sentenced as an adult; we'll treat her as an adult."

"There would be no placement at the juvenile center," Pattison said.

I wasn't about to give up. I drove back to Indianapolis to see DeBruyn. We met over lunch in a state office building cafeteria. He listened to my arguments against housing the juvenile with adults. He seemed sincere about doing what would be in the girl's best interest. He promised to visit the judge, tour the juvenile center in Fort Wayne and interview the girl herself.

Two weeks passed. Then three weeks. Then a whole month. My talk with DeBruyn occurred in January. It was nearly March. As best as I could tell, all he'd done was to meet with McIntosh and Huntington prosecutor Branham. The commissioner did talk briefly with Donna, though the only thing he got out of meeting her was that she didn't look him in the eye.

It dawned on me that the girl needed a new lawyer and a damn good one: DeBruyn and the state of Indiana had no intention of moving the girl to a juvenile center. Now the case took another twist.

JauNae Hanger had worked as an attorney for the state and had run the office of the Indiana Civil Liberties Union where her husband, Rich Waples, served as the chief counsel.

I had just gotten home from an evening meeting when the phone rang. It was JauNae. State Rep. Dennis Avery had told her about Donna. She wanted to hear more. She and her husband wanted to represent Donna. They'd try to get her moved to a juvenile center. Now I saw that the Huntington girl's case might be used as a device to get a change in the law. Yet nutty things happened along the way.

When JauNae visited Donna in the prison for the first time, she discovered the girl had company. There they were, the attorney and her client. That's supposed to be a confidential meeting, right? Apparently not at the Indiana Women's Prison. Superintendent Blank insisted a staff member sit in on the interview. Obviously, the girl wasn't about to tell the full story of how she was being treated at the prison in the presence of a staffer.

JauNae met Donna again as she and her husband got more involved in the case. A couple in their late 30s, they're both tall and good-looking. They live in a gentrified part of the capital, near the downtown. At the time they took Donna's case, they had one son, a toddler.

Over the following months, I talked with both on the phone. Once, I joined them and a law professor from Indiana University for a strategy session over lunch at an Italian restaurant near their home. I mostly listened as the three developed the legal basis for a lawsuit that would challenge Donna's placement.

I came to have great respect for Hanger and Waples. I had never been more impressed by attorneys. It wasn't just their intelligence or knowledge of the law or their hard work. They showed a commitment to civil rights that was genuine, even inspiring. They sure gave their all to Donna. I often told the girl she was lucky to have some of the finest attorneys in Indiana going to bat for her.

With her limited experience, how could she appreciate that?

Not long after that first meeting with Donna, at the ICLU

headquarters, Hanger and Waples announced the lawsuit on the girl's behalf. That sparked a legal battle that would wind up before the Indiana Supreme Court.

That day in December, 1996, when Fox Butterfield's story on Donna's case appeared in The New York Times, I got calls from all over the country. It started at 7 a.m. I had put the prize-winning reporter onto the story. The photograph that went with the article showed this pensive girl, looking down as if in shame. When people saw it they felt so sorry for her they wanted to ride to the rescue. The picture merely served to introduce the tragedy.

Butterfield recounted stories from Donna's sad life. He told of the sexual abuse by family members, the beatings by her mother and how her father, Perry, had denied her and sister Jamie pizza he had brought home.

Butterfield also reported that prison officials wouldn't allow Donna to talk about her own abuse in group therapy. She said that upset the women in the group who had abused their children. Nothing disturbed readers of such accounts more than this.

I did get a different version from prison officials. They brushed aside Donna's claim and said that she was simply told not to call other members in the group names such as "baby killer."

I didn't try to figure out whether it was Donna or the prison officials telling the truth. The girl had such a history of making things up, I sometimes found it hard to separate the fact from the fiction. Yet DOC officials had a vested interest in putting the best face on any report that came out of the prison.

Other inmates, no doubt, resented the extra attention this kid got and the publicity her case attracted. Advocates from around the country. National newspaper stories. Editorials. At one point, ABC's Connie Chung was trying to get into the prison to interview the girl; Gov. O'Bannon nixed that.

Whatever the reason, some inmates threatened Donna. That checked out. The DOC's Pattison told me that was to be expected. I'm also sure women approached her for sex. To be expected in a women's prison, too.

Ted Petti, the Indiana University psychiatrist, spent hours talking with Donna at the prison. He came away with one over-riding impression. Donna was scared to death. My guess was that she kept it together those first few months by telephoning people who had stuck up for her. She had to call collect, although the

DOC limits such calls of inmates to 20 minutes.

Her calls got to be so routine, I knew what day of the week and what time to expect to hear the phone ring.

Invariably, she would call at 9 p.m. on Thursdays, just when PBS' "Mystery!" was about to start. That was my favorite TV show. I always chuckled to myself that the girl sure knew how to get my attention. She'd identify herself, her name seeming to come out of a deep well, flat and unconnected to any real person. But she would greet you warmly, and begin immediately telling you about her new job at the prison or a visit from the Huntington teacher who had tutored her at the county jail.

On a couple of occasions, though, her depression was palpable. She didn't want to go through with the lawsuit. She deserved her punishment. She really loved her mother. She loved Jamie. She wanted to die.

I would listen to this litany of self-loathing, punctuated by sobs, and I'd keep her talking. As soon as the operator came on to tell us we were out of time, I looked up the prison's number, and dialed to report the gist of the conversation. I urged them to keep an eye on her. They did and she didn't come to harm.

From what I've heard and read, it's often hard to pick up the signs of suicide risk in a teenager. Such kids, given the stage of their brain development, can be incredibly impulsive. It's not a subject the staff of an adult prison likely would know much about. As if I needed another reason to oppose putting a kid in an adult prison, I put the risk of suicide on the list.

Likewise, the DOC stumbled on the matter of her schooling. Finally, the Department of Education came up with a retired special education teacher who helped Donna with high school courses. It didn't substitute for instruction from somebody with degrees in math, history and English. But the girl did earn high school credits. (She told me later that the tutor let her peek at the answers in the back of her textbooks.)

I couldn't imagine how the therapy the prison offered could have helped Donna much. Experts who examined her found evidence of half a dozen disorders. She took Prozac for depression. She had a history of bed-wetting as a young teenager—often associated with sexual abuse. Yet for all these problems, Donna only saw a staff psychologist half an hour in biweekly sessions.

Moreover, as the Crossroad psychologist John Link pointed out, you couldn't know what growing up in an adult prison would do to a young teenager, to her way of dealing with other people, to her self-respect, to her view of the world. You probably couldn't collect a worse group of role models for a girl to associate with than those in a women's prison.

Nevertheless, Donna fared better than a lot of kids sent to adult prisons. Nobody beat her that I knew of. She made no overt attempts at suicide. She had friends who seemed to care about her. She had a structure so lacking within her own family.

The next step was back to a courtroom. Now the tone of my editorials on the case shifted from anger back to hope.

Chapter Sixteen

DONNA'S CRIME

Hearing her tell of setting the Grayston Street house on fire always gave me the creeps.

I had seen the photographs the fire marshal's people took of the house and the bodies of her mother and sister. I never have been able to shake the images.

As Donna talked of fetching the can of kerosene from the garage, I pictured the body of Jamie lying only five feet from her bed, her face blackened with soot, her purse lying open at her side.

As Donna told how she started sprinkling the kerosene in the living room, I could see the vacuum sweeper still plugged in. I visualized the black streaks that rose from the baseboards where the fire lapped at the walls.

The note accompanying the photograph says the actual fire was confined to that room.

The couch sat nearby. Perry had been sleeping there just that morning. Now white splotches poked out from the soot that covered most all of the fabric, a useless remnant of the Ratliff household.

I recalled, too, the photograph of the twisted smoke alarm and the note of the investigator that it did not contain the 9-volt battery necessary for the alarm to have alerted her mother and sister to the black peril engulfing every room.

As Donna would describe how, in her rage, she poured kerosene on her collection of stuffed animals, I could see her bed, soot layered over the pillows, sheets and covers gathered in a clump, clothes strewn over the floor.

And I could picture the white wicker chairs in Glissie's bedroom, flowered pillows decorating each one, smoke damage only evident on the legs of one chair.

Donna didn't go to school that Monday. She'd been suspended for hitting a girl on Friday. She walked Jamie to the bus stop, then went home where Perry was asleep on the living room couch. She passed some time playing video games. She stayed indoors. "It was too cold to smoke," she wrote to me.

Glissie had driven her husband's pickup to work; her car was in the shop for repairs.

Donna's ability to recall the day has always seemed uncanny to me. So much of that day seemed so routine. She delivered her weekly newspapers that afternoon, crisscrossing the streets in that working class neighborhood in south Huntington as her dad's friend Robert drove her from one block to the next.

After her mother got home from work, the two argued about whether Donna could visit Perry during his break that evening, which she often did. He worked second shift and wouldn't get home until after 11:30. Glissie said she couldn't go. She went anyway. At the factory, Pyle Industries, Donna and her dad were seen arguing.

Later at home, she and her mother tried to play cards but that erupted into a shouting match. Donna threw her cards at her mother, and Glissie called the social worker, Nanda Wilson, who had often visited the home. But Donna says Nanda wouldn't listen to her. She went to her room, where her plan took shape.

Jamie wasn't around for the argument. Donna says her sister had been drinking and just flopped into bed.

It was well after 10 when Donna was sure her mother and sister both were asleep. With the can of kerosene, she ran through the house, splashing the fluid in two of the bedrooms upstairs and downstairs in the living room, dining room and kitchen. But, she's always insisted, she left the back stairway free of kerosene so her mother and sister had a route of escape.

At the front door, she took her pink-colored Bic lighter from her purse and set the kerosene on fire.

Then, barefoot, wearing only a nightie, she ran next door to the Rabers, but Bob and Hanna didn't answer the door right away, so Donna crossed the street and the family there called 911. The first fire truck arrived four minutes later, at 11:30.

Much of Donna's account in time squares with that of investigators.

Reports of the firefighters describe the smoke being so black they couldn't locate the bodies at first, in fact stumbling over one.

As they brought her mother's body out, Donna said, "Is she dead?" The police and medics observed that she was calm, only mildly curious about her mother's condition.

She first told a police officer that she had heard somebody downstairs and then realized the house was on fire as it quickly filled with smoke. Hurriedly, she tried to awaken Jamie, but her sister was too drunk to wake up. (That claim didn't jibe with the Fort Wayne pathologist's report, which found no alcohol in the blood of either victim.)

So Donna's earliest story quickly unraveled. Medics took Donna to Huntington Memorial Hospital where the emergency room doctor, Patsy Dettimore, swabbed her nostrils and ears. The doctor found no trace of smoke, giving the lie to the girl's account that she had been in the house after the fire started.

As he related it to me, Detective Ron Hochstetler invited Donna to join him on the brown, leatherette couch in the hospital's waiting room.

"I set the fire, I wanted to kill my mother," she blurted out.

Minutes later, Perry, who had followed the ambulance to the hospital, entered and demanded, "I want her prosecuted."

For weeks, until the insurance check came through for Perry, and contractors could begin the repair, the house on Grayston sat empty. Black soot framed the white facade like a shroud. Yellow police tape served to outline the entire property, a reminder to any passerby that he was looking at a crime scene.

"My crime was big," Donna said.

I shuddered to hear of it.

Chapter Seventeen

COURT AGAIN

I shook my head in disbelief. What in the devil was Tom Quigley, the assistant state's attorney, trying to prove? The Indiana Civil Liberties Union's Rich Waples, Donna Ratliff's attorney, put people on the stand in the Marion Superior Court to demonstrate that the girl didn't belong in an adult prison.

It should have been a straightforward matter of fact-finding, determining one way or the other, whether the state constitution required that all juvenile offenders be separated from adult criminals.

That was a legal argument with the authority of Indiana constitutional history plainly on Donna's side.

This time the legal drama was played out in the city-county building taking up a block in downtown Indianapolis. It reminded me of those colorless boxy buildings I saw when I toured Eastern Europe.

With none of the dignified aura of the Huntington court-room, its Marion County counterpart was so purely functional, it might as well have served as a practice basketball gym for inner-city kids.

Judge Patrick McCarty, plainspoken and casual, directed Donna's guard to remove the leg irons from the girl. It was a humane act, even respectful.

But, representing the state, Quigley grilled the witnesses Rich called as if they were implicated in a conspiracy to rob Fort Knox. His manner seemed particularly out of place in the way he interrogated Donna when she got a chance to testify.

The girl, composed, her voice nearly a whisper, guessed she had run away from home three or four times.

Wrong, Quigley shot back. The record shows it was more like 12 times, he said.

He had caught her in a lie. Or at least it sounded as if he did. Perry, the girl's father, sitting in the audience with his arms folded, smiled at her embarrassment. But what did tripping up the girl accomplish? Did it show Donna was a habitual liar? That she couldn't admit her misconduct? That her family was more troubled than she wanted people to know?

No matter why Donna's recollection failed to square with the state's attorney's figures, just how did it add up to a reason she belongs in an adult prison? Or what did any of her presumed lies have to do with whether the state constitution meant what it said about housing juvenile offenders?

In any case, it required a huge leap I couldn't make.

Further on during this hearing, I couldn't fathom why Quigley felt he had to challenge the testimony of Dr. Ted Petti. He actually argued with the psychiatrist. This seemed completely unnecessary.

Petti is a nationally prominent child psychiatrist. He had examined Donna on two occasions after she was sent to the women's prison. He concluded that her fire-setting was a cry for help.

Dr. Petti pointed out that the prison staff had no special training in the treatment of adolescents, especially kids with such a troubled history.

He was outraged that the prison had placed Donna in the special needs unit, which houses physically and mentally disabled women. A terrible setting for her to grow up in, he testified.

He described Donna as depressed, impulsive, hyper-vigilant, even paranoid. But at the time, the special needs unit was about all the women's prison could provide if it was going to protect her from those officials regarded as predators.

"The damage will be irreparable," he warned of keeping Donna at Women's prison.

"She'll only conform to the rules because she's forced to."

Ted's argument was that the highly controlled environment of a prison wouldn't give Donna a chance to develop internal controls. He speculated that, once released, she might well engage again in anti-social behavior.

"Is she amenable to treatment?" Rich Waples asked the doctor.

"Absolutely."

One witness for Donna after another stepped forward to make the case for moving her to a private treatment center.

Barbara Tompkins, a fellow prisoner, testified the girl lived in constant fear of being beaten or sexually molested. The woman had befriended Donna early on. Donna, in turn, had come to think of Barbara as the closest to a real mother she ever had. (As Barbara testified, I'm sure it occurred to a lot of people in the courtroom that this woman, a convicted murderer, hardly represented an ideal role model for a young teenager.)

I was glad to see Rich call Bonnie Shipman to the stand. She headed the English department at the Huntington high school. From the beginning, she had been one of my favorites who took a personal interest in the girl.

She tutored Donna when she was still at the county jail and found the girl "extremely eager to learn." (Through Bonnie's coaching, and that of other Huntington teachers, Donna earned a place on the Huntington North honor roll that fall.)

Bonnie described how Donna had gently fingered her sister's yearbook picture and saw the pain the memory of Jamie had given her. As for the schooling the prison provided for Donna, Bonnie flatly called it "totally inadequate."

Quigley frowned as Bonnie returned to her seat.

Earlier, he had filed a motion to dismiss the case out of hand, arguing that Marion Superior Court Judge Patrick McCarty lacked the authority to reassign anybody in one of the state's prisons. McCarty wasn't buying that.

As I reviewed my notes from that hearing, I was reminded how a psychologist at Girls' School characterized Donna. A prison staffer read the statement that said, "She acted like a 12-year-old and talked only mindless adolescent prattle."

Again, I shook my head in disbelief. Dr. Petti already had testified that the girl was emotionally immature. But it looked as if the state's goal was not to show how the prison could do a good job of rehabilitating her. Only what a hopeless case she was.

So contrary to his intent, Quigley merely demonstrated how much help Donna's rehabilitation required.

Of course, state officials had a pretty good idea where this Donna Ratliff business was headed.

If the courts found Donna's placement violated the state constitution, it meant Indiana's Department of Correction would be forced to build a new center to house the 50 to 100 kids like Donna in the adult prisons at any given time.

So much was at stake for the state.

In his ruling a few days later, Judge McCarty found that the legislature never interpreted the constitution to forbid any commingling of youths and adults in a prison.

Donna called that night, demoralized and ready to drop her lawsuit. I wasn't about to let that idea go any further. At 15, she was too immature to make such a momentous decision. I told her to remember Judge McIntosh's "sincere" recommendation to the DOC. Now the world's authority on the case, he knew where she belonged better than just about anybody.

I insisted she wait and see what would happen to the appeal Rich Waples vowed to make. Could a middle-age journalist confer his own belief that justice eventually prevails on this teenager whose only experience with justice landed her in a maximum security prison?

I was determined to try.

Chapter Eighteen

DONNA'S REDEMPTION

I got so choked up when attorney JauNae Hanger called with the news I could hardly talk.

Months had passed since Donna appeared in the Marion County court. She was now 16.

JauNae gave me the gist of the decision. The Indiana Court of Appeals had ordered Donna Ratliff moved from the women's prison to a suitable private juvenile treatment center.

"Donna wins one," the headline on my editorial the next day announced. The New York Times' Fox Butterfield had himself another story about Donna to write.

I had often reflected on how much her life already had been changed.

Before she set fire to the family home in Huntington, she would have been regarded a lost cause.

After the fire, her life took on a structure it never had. Adults, finally, started to care about what would become of her.

If you looked at her school record, you could have predicted that she would be a dropout. Grades, terrible. Often in fights. Spotty attendance. Attitude? In the toilet. You didn't want to be around her.

If you listened to the stories of her sexual promiscuity, as early as 11 in one report, you'd just know she'd get pregnant. She'd marry young. Following her mom's example, she'd abuse her own kids.

The cycle of abuse in that family would continue on to the next generation, and to the next.

Now consider her life after the fire. Does well in her studies. Earns high school credits. Adapts to structure. Plans for the future. Even in prison, she talks of a career that would let her help other kids in trouble.

To be sure, it took a slew of editorials, a bevy of activists, national publicity, youth counselors and, most important, a lawsuit to turn the Ratliff family tragedy into something hopeful.

Sure, the news Donna would be moved did provoke negative local reaction back in northeast Indiana.

Before the transfer, a Journal Gazette reporter asked Fort Wayne Police Chief Neil Moore what he thought about the state housing this "dangerous young criminal" at Crossroad. Moore said he was dead set against it, although he had never visited the locked unit where Donna would stay.

I made sure he got an invitation to see that unit and take a tour. I had to laugh to myself. The place is so secure the Crossroad staff told the chief he'd have to have his gun locked up. Then, after the tour, with state Rep. Ben GiaQuinta sitting in on our meeting, John Link, the Crossroad psychologist, answered the chief's objections. That was the last complaint I heard about Donna's placement in a juvenile center from anybody.

But the move from the adult prison was only one step on a long journey toward the rehabilitation of a child so insecure and damaged. Months later, I found myself sitting in a lunchroom already decorated for Christmas at Crossroad Children's Home.

The Canada geese you normally could see taking off and landing on the pond and about the rolling campus had taken their winter leave. Low-rolling clouds meant snow couldn't be far behind.

I was listening to the teenage girl across the table telling me, matter-of-factly, about swallowing a piece of metal she'd ripped off a Christmas card and how the x-ray they did at the hospital showed the sharp edge of the metal had done no damage.

The Crossroad psychiatrist, Dr. Sylvia Manalis, explained that teenage girls often cut themselves or swallow something that could hurt them as a way to cope with severe stress and depression.

Donna didn't seem depressed the day she told me she swallowed the metal piece off a greeting card. But by the time of that visit, Dr. Manalis, whose specialty was kids, had upped the girl's Prozac. Troubled kids, being who they are, ride a lot of ups and downs. But Donna got more ups at Crossroad than she had at the prison.

It only took me a few weekly visits before I began to see the transformation. She smiled. She laughed. She joked. She held her head up. Those blue eyes of hers looked straight at you. No head hanging shamefully down. She bragged about her grades with Janice, her full-time teacher.

In prison, her private therapy consisted of half-hour sessions twice a month. At Crossroad, she met for an hour or more with her therapist, Laurie Evans, nearly every day.

She got a reputation at the center of looking out for other girls.

Link told me that in his more than 20 years dealing with such kids, he found Donna had become the most insightful and promising of any.

Now she had more visitors, more frequently. She could count on seeing friends from Huntington each week. A Fort Wayne minister she thought of as "Grandpa" brought her treats and stuffed animals. He drove the 20 miles to Huntington to photograph the grave sites of Donna's mother and sister. (Seeing the pictures would aid in her therapy Laurie, her counselor, explained.)

At Crossroad, Donna's adult role models weren't criminals who might even be mentally ill. They were responsible adults trained in dealing with screwed up kids. They cared about Donna, and it showed. Donna trusted them. That showed, too.

Crossroad meant Donna associated with other teenagers. She had to learn how to get along.

"That yelling is driving me crazy," she complained the first few weeks. Back in the prison, the guards had kept things nice and quiet, order being the prevailing ethos. Link pointed out that she had to learn to deal with the racket. Otherwise, he asked, "How do you expect her to deal with a screaming baby when she becomes a mother?"

I thought the new DOC Commissioner, Ed Cohn, got carried away with the oversight from afar. I suppose the publicity over the case spooked this veteran prison bureaucrat. Anyway, he demanded that everything that Donna did be included in a regular report to him. Once, when she painted a staff member's handcuffs with fingernail polish, Cohn said she had to clean off the polish.

He did permit a young woman working for a New York production company to interview Donna for a National Public Radio special on kids in adult prisons, titled "If I Get Out Alive." I sat in on the interview as Tracey Barry got Donna to talk about her experience, her fear of certain guards, her sense of hopelessness, her constant sense of being out of place.

More than 200 NPR affiliates aired the hour-long program, narrated by Diane Keaton, and millions more people got to know the sad story of the girl from Huntington, Indiana.

Nor did Cohn object when I lined up visits for Donna to my own dentist in Fort Wayne, a personal friend, Dr. Keith Yoder.

Keith found Donna's teeth had been terribly neglected at the DOC and scheduled a number of appointments. I was so thankful her dental care was getting the attention it needed. Few things can make a teenager more self-conscious than bad teeth.

One theme that ran through many of my conversations was her dad. She blamed him for somehow giving her the idea to set the fire, although she gave conflicting accounts of how that happened. Yet both Perry and his daughter seemed eager for reconciliation. They met once at Crossroad. After that, Perry told me Donna's accusations were just crazy. I never knew what to think. Despite that cloud, the girl's healing at Crossroad went on.

In the more than two years she spent at Crossroad, the staff helped host a couple of Christmas parties for her friends. People from Huntington showed up. JauNae Hanger brought her boy to one party. The Fort Wayne minister and his family came with some church members in tow. My wife Toni and I brought hot yeast rolls. Somebody had fixed Donna's hair and it made her look older than the girl she was.

She wore a purple party dress and heels, and jabbered and joked the evening away. As the party wound down, she stood to give a touching speech about how she'd never before been in a place where everybody loved her.

"I am very blessed," she said.

At that moment, I was able to forget about the fire and the grotesque photographs of the tragedy that sat in the files of my study at home. Meantime, things weren't going so well for the cause on the legal front.

The Indiana Supreme Court overturned the appeals court's finding that housing kids in adult prisons violated the state constitution. The high court left the matter in the hands of the General Assembly. I was disappointed but not surprised. I had attended the court's hearing. And the justices' questions showed they weren't buying the constitutional argument.

Nevertheless, Commissioner Cohn said Donna could stay at Crossroad until she graduated from high school that June.

Graduate she did. Like most all of the center's kids, she was treated as a student of Fort Wayne Community Schools. She graduated in the top third of her North Side High School class. She had turned 18 in February.

I met with Gov. O'Bannon and appealed to him, as a fellow grandfather, to allow the girl to remain at Crossroad until she was 21. The governor didn't commit himself, which I took as a bad sign.

No dice, Cohn told me later. Donna was headed back to prison once she graduated. It was midsummer, though, before the DOC got around to moving her. But this wasn't the trauma that her first trip to the prison, at 14, represented for Donna.

She was ready to go. She had become an adult, though certainly one who still needed to come to terms with the terrible burden of abuse and the guilt she felt for being her mother and sister's killer.

I didn't hear much from her after her return to the women's prison. No more regular calls during my favorite television shows. I stopped by for a visit each time I was in Indianapolis. Mostly, she talked about her college studies, which she commenced soon after she got back to the prison. Ball State University professors drove down to the prison from Muncie and offered courses leading to a degree in general studies.

Three years later, prison officials held a college graduation ceremony for Donna. Again, she invited her friends. Even the DOC commissioner was on hand to congratulate her. Earning the degree meant she'd be entitled to be released on probation early.

As she was about to be released, I visited Judge McIntosh in his chambers back at the Huntington courthouse. I think he'd lost track of Donna by then. I wondered what he'd say when he learned that because of her "good time" and college she would have served little more than seven years of the 25-year sentence he originally had imposed.

But when I announced that she was getting out, he smiled and shook my hand warmly.

"Larry, you know I think we've done just about everything we can for this girl."

End of story for him, I thought. For Donna, just another beginning.

Chapter Nineteen

MISS CORESSEL

In the fourth grade, I became an authority on how teachers ought to treat their students.

Looking back, I'm surprised I didn't share this wisdom more often with readers of my editorials.

I sure did crank out a lot of pieces on schools. I denounced standardized testing, paddling, segregation, chintzy budgets, stupid spelling lists and algebra. In turn, I lauded a bunch of other stuff.

As a rule, I could cite research I picked up from interviews with academics or from those I heard speak at the Education Writers Association's conferences.

At one time or another, I got around to every conceivable school topic. But I'm silent, with rare exceptions, about what I regard as the most important thing in schools. Here it is:

A teacher must treat each child with simple respect.

If I had a magic wand, I would make threats, scoldings and arbitrary, mindless punishments disappear from every classroom. I've known what I'm talking about for a long time. As I said, as far back as fourth grade.

Slocum Elementary provided the scene of my enlightenment. The year was 1947 or thereabouts. Most of my best friends attended that school in Defiance, Ohio, my home town. The kids were the sons and daughters of doctors, dentists and lawyers, as well as janitors, grocery store clerks and the salesman who peddled supplies to barbers.

My family had one foot in poverty and one planted among the town's country club set. So they were uncertain of their social status. And I never could be sure where I stood in my classmates' eyes. More than anything, I longed for their respect. And the teacher's.

My goal in life at that time, sadly, was not a priority for Miss Helena Coressel.

The day of my humiliation started innocently enough. She

drilled us on the multiplication tables. No sweat. Of course, we'd had the same drill the day before.

Then she assigned us a page to copy on Egypt from our geography text. (I suppose she needed time to herself to grade papers at her desk.) I balked at the assignment. I asked whether it wouldn't be OK if we just read the thing. If I sounded snotty I didn't mean to.

Her face reddened, which it did easily anyway, her being of fair complexion and a natural blonde. She declared that my question showed that I was acting like a kindergartner.

In high school, my young English teacher, who years later became a friend, ordered me to write on the chalkboard 100 times the phrase, "I will not be impertinent." You easily can guess what that was all about.

But back in fourth grade, my punishment for the infraction required that I be sent to the kindergarten room. I was to spend the rest of the morning there and presumably would ponder the early flowering of impertinence.

So down two flights of steps I stumbled toward the kindergarten room and my moral execution at the bottom of the stairs. The teacher placed a tiny chair for me in the corner next to the doorway; I was to be humiliated before her class as well as my own.

Within minutes, time came for phys. ed., and my class trooped single-file down the stairs toward the school gym, right past the kindergarten room, each classmate taking note of my nine-year-old presence among the five-year-olds.

Miss Lind, my first-grade teacher and Slocum's principal, stopped by the kindergarten room, saw me in the tiny red wooden chair, and took it upon herself to give me a further scolding, with the ominous prediction, "Wait till your mother hears about this."

Of course, I had no chance to defend my conduct, just as I had no idea that declining to copy a page on Egypt out of my textbook could rain down such wrath upon my little curly head.

The lesson that stuck, it turned out, had nothing to do with Egypt. But then, teachers don't always appreciate that kids learn lessons they weren't teaching. This time, I witnessed the perils of questioning authority. I pondered that long after I stopped nursing my hurt.

Moreover, I had been thoughtlessly, needlessly humiliated. For a time, such punishment no doubt had shaken my confidence.

Don't tell me it fired me up to study the geography of the Mideast. Forget that.

I'm sure it wasn't the teacher's intent to hurt me. She certainly didn't mean to kill my enthusiasm for an education. Nevertheless, I came to see her as a cruel person, not my ally in that great adventure of learning.

I doubt that Miss Coressel was the only teacher at Slocum who mistakenly believed that humiliating a student would be a terrific motivator. Or, maybe she just resented that a kid had challenged her judgment. But how can such treatment have any other outcome than to alienate the student?

Which leads me to my crusade against paddling in schools.

Family album

In Defiance, I'm geared up for the NFL season

Chapter Twenty

SPARE THE CHILD

It was a terrible night. Blustery outside, and cold as the devil. I couldn't sleep. I rolled and tossed, ruminating about how it was still legal for teachers and principals to paddle school children.

In less than two days, newly elected school board members, more conservative, would replace appointed ones. My hopes to get the practice of paddling in the schools banned would diminish further.

I often felt like the Lone Ranger on this cause, though I knew that wasn't the case. State Rep. John Day, a Democrat, introduced a bill to ban paddling every year. Professor Lawrence Beymer of Indiana State University used to write letters to the editor and articles about his research to show the prevalence of the practice.

Beymer once remarked how ironic it was that in some districts teachers were told not to hug kids but they could pull a kid's pants down and paddle his bottom. Doubly ironic, state law permitted the paddling of school children but forbade corporal punishment of prisoners of any age.

But here I was with this terrific platform from which to denounce the legalized abuse of children. That was how I felt about it. Yet I had zilch to show for my passionate advocacy.

That night, one image I couldn't get out of my mind was something I heard about from Beth Sheets, a teacher and a good friend. Her daughter Sarah was just starting her teaching career as a substitute.

It was a few months before the district's desegregation settlement, in 1989. Sarah had been called to fill in at an inner-city, predominately black school. She hardly had gotten settled taking attendance when the African-American principal entered the classroom and led one particularly cute boy out.

A few minutes later, the principal returned with the boy.

The kid was in tears and held his backside. The young teacher didn't need a spy in the principal's office to figure out what had happened. The boy had been paddled.

Sarah protested that he had done nothing wrong. The principal replied that he meant to see that the boy wouldn't act up for the substitute.

I had heard lots of horror stories from around the Midwest about paddling for all sorts of minor offenses. A middle schooler forgets to discard his chewing gum. A first-grader underlines answers on a worksheet instead of circling them as the teacher instructed. Even today, swearing can get a kid paddled at the middle school my granddaughters attend, in a small, northeastern Indiana community.

My editorials on paddling focused on the harm it can inflict on children. My favorite authority was Temple University's Irving Hyman. He had spent his career studying the issue. He found that corporal punishment often does lifelong damage. In writing about Hyman's research, I also noted the international trend to outlaw the practice even in the home.

I also reminded school officials how excessive paddling could invite costly lawsuits.

But I couldn't get a rise. I tried teachers' union officials, both state and local. No, although they might personally agree with me, they couldn't support a ban on paddling.

Teachers, it seemed, insisted on keeping corporal punishment as an option, "the club in the closet," state Rep. Barbara Engle, an area high school teacher, called it. Fort Wayne Community Schools Superintendent Bill Anthis told me any change would have to come from the board.

I had at least one ally on the board in the early days of my crusade. That was Dr. Bernie Stuart, an African-American dentist. For him to object to corporal punishment in itself was noteworthy. Many black parents regard paddling as not only their right but their duty. I had tangled with black professionals who defended paddling as just part of the culture.

Indeed, it was my impression Bernie's quarrel wasn't so much with paddling. It was the fact most of the kids getting paddled were black, according to a survey of Fort Wayne schools by the U.S. Office for Civil Rights.

That sleepless night, it occurred to me that Sarah's story was the first time I'd heard about a kid getting paddled to prevent misbehavior—a preemptive strike in the schoolroom.

Replaying this scenario in my mind, and building up a fair amount of anger, I finally got up, half-awake, and stumbled to the bathroom. When I returned, I had a plan. In the morning, I would call Stan Lipp.

You need to know a couple of things about Stan. He was one of the appointed members who would be going off the board Monday. Stan owned a carpet store on the north side of town so mammoth you could have held a rock concert in it. An acquaintance of mine for years, he'd always come across as a typical Midwestern businessman, outgoing, politically moderate and civic-minded.

His most visible political role came when he served as campaign manager for our Democratic mayor, Win Moses, Jr. Stan was an active member of the Jewish temple, his wife a teacher in one of the suburban districts.

Most important, Stan was a vocal though not abrasive board member. He urged the district to be more open. He even proposed that school officials conduct negotiations with the teachers' union in public. But that was Stan, always wanting the schools to be responsive to parents and other citizens. Unfortunately, as I said, he was leaving the board.

He answered the phone right away, listening to my concern. As a matter of fact, he agreed with me, he said. Without further discussion—I was prepared to recite a catalogue of arguments against paddling—he promised to see what he could do and get back to me. It was one of the longest weekends of my life.

My wife's parents were coming for dinner. That took my mind off my corporal punishment obsession. I knew my father-in-law wouldn't agree with me, so I didn't bring up the topic. Just as my wife started to serve dessert, the phone rang. I stepped out of the dining room and picked up the kitchen phone. It was Stan.

"Well, it's done," he said. I recall, in fact, that was all he said. But I got the message: He had lined up the votes to ban paddling in Fort Wayne Community Schools. That night, I slept like a baby.

The next day came the board meeting. That not only marked the end of an era for mayoral and township trustee appointments. In the middle of the meeting, a policy bombshell exploded, something I had helped plant.

Superintendent Bill Anthis praised the outgoing board

members, including my corporal punishment ally Stan Lipp, Bernie Stuart and Dr. Jeff Towles, who had broken ranks with Anthis over school desegregation.

Anthis presented each with a plaque to honor their years of service. He observed that the retirement of this group represented the greatest loss of experience the district ever witnessed at one time. I figured that in his heart the superintendent was relieved to see them go.

As it turned out, the resolution to ban paddling was only a bombshell for the superintendent, teachers, their union and the media, not including me of course. It was no surprise to board members, since Stan had already lined up the votes to pass his proposal.

Minutes of that mid-December meeting show the board spent "considerable time" discussing corporal punishment. To my memory, that discussion was another first of that school board meeting. However, the superintendent didn't see fit to take note of it.

Stan wanted the new policy to not only ban paddling but all forms of corporal punishment and to apply to all grades. One member proposed that the board amend the resolution to require the district to develop alternatives to discipline. That was done, unanimously. Then the amended resolution passed, with only one dissenting vote.

Next day, the news stories quoted union officials who complained that they hadn't been consulted about the policy change. In fact, the stories mentioned how Stan Lipp's proposal seemed to "come out of nowhere." My editorial lavished praise on the board, with no hint of my role.

Now, more than a decade later, hundreds more school districts throughout the country have abolished corporal punishment. It is banned in 28 states. While paddling remains legal in Indiana, Professor Beymer, now retired, reminds me the practice has nearly died out.

Meantime, I can only speculate about the number of people in our state who still carry the emotional scars inflicted upon them in their school days long ago. But when somebody tells me he was paddled a lot as a kid and it didn't hurt him, I realize it would be a waste of breath to dispute the person. I certainly don't cite the decades of research that show corporal punishment can scar a person for life.

I just figure the person is lucky to have found a way to forgive the humiliation. Or else is in denial.

Chapter Twenty-One

THE DAY JIM CROW DIED

Nothing defined my career writing editorials better than my crusade to see Fort Wayne Community Schools desegregate its elementary schools.

Most people, including two superintendents and key board members, opposed so dramatic a change. It was a tough sell.

That's why the battle lasted so long. Maybe 20 years. Of course, the bigots in town didn't want little black and white kids in school together. It was no use trying to convert them.

But another bunch of folk just felt that kids did better in neighborhood schools. With the school close, parents are more likely to get involved, they said. True. But I've never found any evidence that kids learn more in a neighborhood school than one they're bused to. (People may not be aware of it, but over 60 percent of students in this country go to school on a bus.)

We had one particular case that proved to be an obstacle. This was Bunche Elementary. The principal was Oscar Underwood. He and the school enjoyed a great deal of popularity in the black community. Oscar also served as the minister to some of the families whose kids attended Bunche.

Oscar had been a good friend since he taught my daughter in fifth and sixth grade in a suburban district. Those classes were racially mixed. But, years later, leading this inner-city school, he fought the change. Superintendent Bill Anthis brought him to a meeting with the paper's editorial board so this gifted educator could persuade us that his school should remain as it was.

I wasn't going to be put in the position of saying an all-black school couldn't do a decent job of teaching the kids. But in that meeting I pointed out that Fort Wayne Community Schools had only one principal as inspiring and talented as Oscar

Underwood. "Where are the others?" I asked. Our guests had no answer. Events would soon overtake such discussions anyway.

Once a biracial group of parents sued the schools, once the thing got into federal court, once school officials saw their defense was futile, the law of the land plopped down like a lost bald eagle in northeast Indiana.

The deal followed months of bitter negotiations. People got mad and stalked out. They pointed their fingers in other people's faces and slammed their fists on the table. Sometimes, they even refused to meet. I heard all this second-hand.

Somehow, the two sides struck a deal. The announcement came in February, 1989, a momentous day if I say so myself.

Here was this conservative city, where blacks were supposed to know their place, about to become a national success story as one of the few racially balanced urban districts in the country. I had invested a big chunk of my life in the battle.

To me, desegregating the schools was not only morally right. It was an educational imperative.

So I badgered scores of people who already had enough grief in their lives. I went to meetings at schools and churches. I hung out with other civil rights buffs so I didn't feel like Don Quixote on this subject. I stuffed our attic with my notebooks of scribblings on the subject. The big payoff had arrived. Sweet Jesus, sweet justice.

Chapter Twenty-Two

FREEDOM'S SLOW TRAIN

By the time civil rights rumbled into Fort Wayne, in February, 1989, the performers were too pooped and bedraggled to put on much of a show. Twenty-year runs do that to a person and to a cause.

Back in the fall of 1969, black preachers organized a boycott of the schools. They demanded justice. That was the year I came back to the city from Cincinnati to teach high school English. The boycott kept 1,500 kids out of school for more than a week. Volunteers taught them in storefront churches transformed into freedom schools.

The preachers thought they had old Pharaoh by the throat. But the city's two newspapers buried the story on the inside pages. Neither one bothered to editorialize the entire 10 days of the boycott. (I was still teaching.)

Well, no surprise, it collapsed. Old Pharaoh, otherwise known as Superintendent Lester Grile, promised to fix the problem. All the ministers got for their trouble was one magnet school. Which, oddly, seemed to give preference to the families of the rich and powerful.

Ninety-eight-point-three percent, or thereabouts, of the black kids stayed stuck in those same black schools. Jump ahead a couple of years.

In 1971, the officials opened two new high schools and closed old Central, which had become predominately black. The result was that the secondary schools ended up racially balanced.

How dumb, I said to a lot of people, to integrate older kids whose racial attitudes had hardened and leave the younger kids in 27 of 36 elementary schools that were "extremely racially isolated," according to the U.S. Office of Civil Rights.

When I joined the paper in late 1973, I had become obsessed with the desegregation cause. I drove my friends nuts complaining about school officials and arguing the benefits of desegregation.

Now, mounting my soapbox on the editorial page, I had an audience of thousands to preach to daily. In my zeal, I wasn't always fair or even nice. I offended some people that I didn't need to, although I never explicitly accused anybody of racism.

For a time, I bypassed otherwise willing allies. I probably sounded sanctimonious, at least that's what Bishop John D'Arcy told me. (Of course when you're right, you're right.)

By the late 1980s, the filing of a lawsuit in federal court did what no huffing and puffing on my part could accomplish. Even then, we all duked it out a couple more years.

Finally, with a nasty, divisive trial looming, not to mention a lot of pressure from U.S. District Judge Allen Sharp, attorneys for the school district and PQEI—Parents for Quality Education with Integration—found common ground over details and reached a settlement. A trial was averted.

The news that cold day in February stopped history. Segregation in our schools turned to dust. The walls of Jericho could not have fallen harder. It took an army of Joshuas to get the job done, though.

Chapter Twenty-Three

IAN AND ME

Abraham Lincoln looked on as Ian and I hatched the plot.

Lincoln freed the slaves. Now he could inspire us to liberate black children from segregated schools in Fort Wayne. Here was my role in the story.

I never ran out of passion for the issue. But over time I calculated that I wasn't going to change the hearts and minds of school officials on my desegregation crusade.

By the 1980s, Bill Anthis had succeeded Lester Grile as superintendent. While I had come to see Anthis as more progressive, it became clear that neither he nor board members had the imagination and the courage to shut down the all-black elementary schools. I turned to other civil leaders. I didn't so much invoke the educational or legal case for desegregation. I appealed to their sense of pride about the city.

I saw a powerful connection between our neglect of black children and the city's well-being. The refusal to desegregate the elementary schools, I argued in one editorial, was a stain on the city's reputation.

After the flood of 1982, Fort Wayne's image-makers dubbed us "the city that saved itself." Yes, I said in what turned out to be a fateful editorial, we may have saved ourselves from worse flood damage than we did have. Good for us.

But were we losing our soul because the school district refused to end the racial isolation of black children? Moreover, the racial taint of the school district made our leaders look like legendary segregationists such as Lester Maddox and Bull Connor to the rest of the country. (This part I probably stretched a bit.)

Fort Wayne's heaviest hitter of all heard me.

The day the editorial ran I called Ian Rolland, head of Lincoln National Corporation. What did he think? Surely he agreed. I hoped he'd get involved. Maybe even beat a couple of board members to a pulp. What he did was better than that. And quite legal.

For much of his tenure as Lincoln's CEO, we all knew him as the city's most influential and most progressive business leader. It wasn't just for his racial attitudes, either. He was the first corporate boss to ban smoking in the workplace. He saw to it that gays could put their partners on the company health insurance policy.

That day, he and I huddled in his office on the top floor of the old Lincoln Life Insurance building on Harrison Street in Fort Wayne's downtown. A dark brown, wooden bust of Abraham Lincoln at Ian's elbow looked on. Maybe it was my imagination. But I thought Abe looked pleased.

Rolland came right to the point.

His public persona was one of the wise, earnest diplomat. In photographs, he often flashes a winning smile. In private he can be blunt as an army drill instructor. In this meeting, he was furious. He said he was outraged that the superintendent and board members continued to evade their clear responsibility to desegregate.

For a minute, he looked so stern I thought he might be mad at me.

I outlined the gist of the February, 1984, "Statement of Findings" by the U.S. Office for Civil Rights. OCR found the district had 27 elementary schools that were "extremely racially imbalanced." That was the vast majority of the elementaries. Mind you, the feds put out that report during the Reagan administration.

I summarized the report for Ian, showing how for generations school officials had contrived to keep black kids in one group of schools racially isolated, separated from white kids. The discrimination was often blatant. No doubt about it, the segregation had been on purpose.

One example I recall mentioning was how black elementary children were once housed at predominately black Central High School, despite the fact these kids lived closer to a white elementary that had enough vacant space to house a mid-size department store.

Such conscious segregation created the basis for a lawsuit against the district. "A classic case," Gary Orfield, the nation's preeminent desegregation expert told me, after he had read OCR's report. Rolland got the message faster than I could spell it out.

I further told him how futile my private talks with Anthis

had been. I explained how the fears of white flight and political fallout had paralyzed district officials. I also wondered aloud whether racial prejudice lay behind much of the resistance.

At the least, I didn't believe most board members grasped the damage racial isolation was doing to children, black and white. I sized up the school board members one by one, giving Ian my assessment of each one's willingness to negotiate in good faith and avert an ugly and protracted court battle.

In the weeks that followed, I met frequently with Rolland. Weekends, we had breakfast together at a Richard's Restaurant on the city's west side. He often would show up in his jogging suit, sweaty from his morning run. We'd fill up on coffee and pecan waffles smothered in maple syrup and plot negotiating strategy.

During those confabs, I learned more of Ian's history, how in the 1960s a United Methodist minister, the Reverend A. Hunter Colpitts, had challenged him to see the plight of poor blacks and how that minister helped transform Ian's own racial attitudes.

It wasn't long before Ian led the church group to establish the East Wayne Street Center, a social agency in one of the city's most segregated neighborhoods. He and his wife Miriam adopted a black daughter.

As our breakfast meetings went on, Rolland wanted the names and telephone numbers of experts and those of civil rights attorneys. That hardly was a problem. Given all the years I had been championing desegregation, there were few authorities I hadn't interviewed over the phone or in person.

I named my favorite researchers, Orfield, then at the University of Chicago, Christine Rossell at Boston University, Bob Crane at Johns Hopkins, Charles Willie at Harvard, Willis Hawley at Vanderbilt's Peabody Teachers College, Janet Schofield at the University of Pittsburgh.

What I learned from these folk, I shared. For one thing, the federal courts had been saying this: Northern school districts that had a history of assigning students on the basis of race had opened themselves to lawsuits. At issue was whether such districts had violated the 14th Amendment's equal protection clause.

Naturally, Rolland and I discussed the Supreme Court's 1954 landmark decision. That ruling concluded that separate schools for black children were inherently unequal. To be sure, school officials here insisted they were spending the same amount of money on black schools as they did on white schools. But merely spending the money on black schools didn't cut it.

Study after study showed that teachers in all-black schools expected less of the kids, who, in turn expected less of them-selves. Moreover, separating them from white children engendered feelings of inferiority in the black kids. No matter how you wanted to slice it, dumping most of these kids in a few, inner-city schools added up to a raw academic deal.

Year after year, consistently poor test scores told the story. If school officials refused to do anything about it, there was only one option: a lawsuit.

As he listened to me carry on about the problems of segregated schools, Rolland announced he wanted to hear more about Bill Taylor, the Washington, D.C., civil rights attorney. I gladly obliged. Now, as Dad would have said, we were cooking with gas.

Courtesy The Journal Gazette

Ian Rolland, Fort Wayne's most influential civic leader

Chapter Twenty-Four

MR. TAYLOR, ESQ.

I had this fantasy. Thurgood Marshall would take a leave of absence from the U.S. Supreme Court. He'd come to Fort Wayne to argue the desegregation case on behalf of the black children of our city. He'd get the job done just as he did in the landmark Brown vs. Board of Education case, more than a generation before.

But a civil rights attorney that I came to respect as much as Marshall was Bill Taylor. He not only had the intelligence and an encyclopedic knowledge of the history of school desegregation. He felt that same righteous indignation over segregated schools that I associated with our first black Supreme Court justice. Taylor had tutored rookie civil rights attorneys in the movement. He spoke with authority on the subject, having played a big part in it.

When Taylor is stirred to lay out an argument on behalf of his cause, he makes it with eloquence and passion.

As a young attorney under Marshall at the NAACP Legal Defense Fund, he drafted the brief in the Little Rock desegregation case. Later, Lyndon Johnson appointed him staff director of the U.S. Civil Rights Commission.

No doubt about it, Taylor would be ideal to take charge of the Fort Wayne desegregation case. It's in precisely such cases as St. Louis and Cincinnati, where his skills both in the courtroom and at backroom negotiations would be called for.

Walter Rice, the U.S. District judge in the Cincinnati case, told me he admired no attorney more than Taylor and "often wished he could be cloned."

No wonder the Northern Indiana District judge in the Fort Wayne court accorded a deference to Taylor that I didn't see him show the Fort Wayne or the state attorneys.

I valued Taylor for his patience with me during phone interviews. He answered all questions about the history of desegregation lawsuits and court rulings. If he had to rush to a meeting, he'd promise to call back later. He kept his promise, too.

Later, I'd see Taylor in a more complete light when he invited me to join him for a strategy session in Washington, D.C. Activists at the offices of the People For The American Way were plotting to fight the expected nomination of conservative Sen. Orrin Hatch to the Supreme Court.

Others spoke in turn, mostly chattering and sometimes not listening to those on the other side of the table. Sitting next to me, Taylor said little but remained attentive. As the discussion wound down, however, everyone turned to the civil rights giant. There was no murmuring then.

Taylor summed up the plan, who would do the research on Hatch, what direction that would take, and what senators would be contacted first. Hatch was never nominated. But another conservative, former Solicitor General Robert Bork was. A chief strategist behind the defeat of that nomination was none other than Bill Taylor.

Ian Rolland and others from Fort Wayne finally met him in the fall of 1985. We gathered in Taylor's unpretentious Washington offices, just a healthy walk north of the White House. I wondered what kind of impression Taylor would make on Rolland.

Tall, with dark, penetrating brown eyes that darted from one of his Fort Wayne visitors to the next, Taylor was all business. At that moment, this chain-smoker, dressed in an unremarkable grey suit, on the verge of disheveled, was trying to get off cigarettes and was chewing Wrigley's Doublemint to beat the band. Taylor was an attorney not at all like the Brooks Brothers types in Lincoln's corporate offices.

But Rolland already had his community outreach expert, LaDonna Huntley-James, check out Taylor's resume and Rolland came right to the point—the matter of a desegregation lawsuit against Fort Wayne Community Schools.

"How much will it cost to get us started?"

"About $100,000," Taylor answered.

Rolland was standing just a foot or so from me. He didn't flinch at this pricey piece of community activism or hesitate with his reply. There wasn't even a pause between Taylor's statement and Rolland's reply, as if the statements of the two men were one sentence uttered by the same person.

"OK, let's go ahead," Rolland said.

The Fort Wayne school desegregation story had just taken a dramatic turn.

Courtesy The Journal Gazette

My civil rights hero, Bill Taylor

Chapter Twenty-Five

SUPERINTENDENT'S WING-TIPS

I sure understood why Superintendent Bill Anthis wasn't eager to meet with me yet one more time. If he'd had his fill of my editorials criticizing him, I wouldn't have been surprised. So our first words had nothing to do with desegregation. Rather, we talked about his shoes, about the brown, wing-tip Florsheims he always wore.

I have no idea how this subject came up.

But this tiny, seemingly irrelevant fact told you a lot about the superintendent. This was a person who liked routine, a life of no surprises. Don't ask him to switch brands of shoes. And he'd prefer you not ask him to do more to integrate the schools than he already had, by moving the sixth-grade kids into racially balanced middle schools.

Ian Rolland hoped bringing a civil rights giant into the case would persuade Anthis and board members to negotiate an agreement to end the racial isolation. Nobody was eager to file a lawsuit. That would be sure to draw unflattering attention to Fort Wayne. In particular, Rolland feared the lawsuit would aggravate community divisions festering since the black boycott of the elementary schools in 1969.

My editorials at that point reflected Rolland's caution. I nagged, but I didn't blast anybody. Though I dearly wanted to.

For all the flak I took—and had generously dished out over the years—I maintained cordial if sometimes strained relations with Anthis and board members, even as the desegregation battle was about to move into the federal court.

I bent over backwards to be fair. Well, that's the way it seemed to me.

Board member Dick Doermer, a highly regarded banker in

town, submitted a lengthy op. ed. piece, justifying the FWCS position. I thought the piece neatly ignored the main issue: the perpetuation of racial injustice. Yet I saw that the piece got priority attention, and we ran it on the Sunday op. ed. page.

Our watchword at the paper was to be fair. No exceptions. We would have printed Stalin's letters defending the Gulag.

To hear the concerns of Anthis and Doermer, and, I hoped, to coax them to give a fresh look at racial balance, I met them one morning over a lengthy breakfast. When I arrived, Anthis was waiting alone in a meeting room on the 13th floor of the Summit Square office building.

From that vantage point, you could see one of the city's three rivers below, threading through the downtown. Just off on the horizon, you could spot the dark red brick building of long-ago racially balanced North Side High School, where Anthis once presided as principal.

He gave me a perfunctory greeting. Then we got to talking about his wing-tips. It was a weird conversation.

When the subject did turn to racial balance, Anthis, with some embarrassment, I thought, said that he couldn't just issue a policy on his own but had to take direction from the board, often split. Was he really as resistant to change as I thought?

Joining us, Doermer, ever affable, steered the conversation in the direction of his overriding fear—white flight.

I cited the research of Chris Rossell of Boston University. She found white flight occurred in anticipation of desegregation, not as a result. It was their maneuvering and delays, I argued, that would prompt white parents to abandon the urban school district for the suburbs. They listened politely. Clearly, they weren't buying my argument.

Weeks later, Rolland had a go at it. Rolland's thinking was, win over such a respected figure on or off the board as Doermer, and you win the battle for desegregation. With that hope in mind, Rolland invited the retired News-Sentinel editor, Ernie Williams, Doermer and a couple of others to join him on Lincoln's corporate jet.

The destination was Chicago, where the Fort Wayne group would meet the desegregation expert Gary Orfield, then a University of Chicago political science professor, plus a Seattle business executive and school board president who had backed desegregation in his city earlier in the decade.

In a visit to his home later, Williams told me he declined the invitation, felt it was pointless trying to change Doermer's mind and, besides, "At my age, I don't do anything I don't feel like any more."
Williams' prophecy was dead on. But if anything, Doermer's inflexibility only made Rolland more committed than ever. Further, the meeting with Orfield left Rolland better educated about school desegregation.

It would have been understandable if Doermer's unspoken agenda was to protect his business, Summit Bank, from any adverse community reaction to desegregation. He never expressed that fear to me. In fairness to Doermer, it should be noted Rolland himself remained insulated from such a problem.

Indeed, as Rolland readily acknowledged, most of Lincoln's insurance and investment clients didn't live in Fort Wayne.

I urged school officials to bring major desegregation experts to the city, to get their advice and to let them assuage fears of citizens. In one response, Anthis invited Charles Willie of Harvard to Fort Wayne. Willie had designed Cambridge's plan, known as "controlled choice," which racially balanced the schools in that city within each attendance area, rather than district-wide. I had spoken with the Little Rock superintendent who had introduced controlled choice in his city, as well. He sounded delighted with the results.

The idea had merit for Fort Wayne. But the only remark about Willie I heard from any school official came from one of the smartest and dearest men in the FWCS hierarchy, Associate Superintendent John Young. During Willie's talk, John learned over to me and whispered that the Harvard professor looked a lot like Willie Mays.

For a time, such outside experts paraded in and out of the city. Meantime, Bill Taylor and Rolland had been quietly enlisting black and white parents to organize into a group that would represent children damaged by segregated schools if a lawsuit were filed. This group became Parents for Quality Education with Integration, PQEI.

Still, I hadn't lost hope some outside expert would break the logjam here. About the time FWCS officials were trying to fend off a lawsuit, Mayor Win Moses, Jr. hosted a conference on desegregation, bringing national figures to share their views.

Echoing the views of various speakers, Chris Rossell of Boston University talked up magnet schools, the specialty of her research. Jay Robinson, superintendent of the Charlotte-Mecklenburg district in North Carolina, argued the case for desegregation—including the social and academic benefits that grew out of his city's court-ordered busing.

The sour note of that conference came from James Meredith. He was the courageous black student who integrated Old Miss but in recent years had become disenchanted with racial integration.

In his speech, Meredith claimed desegregation was a fraud that would hurt black students more than it would help them. One of the few people who warmly applauded the speech was Anthis, the superintendent.

He took his embrace of Meredith further. He saw to it that board members who didn't attend the conference got a copy of Meredith's speech but not copies of the speeches by those experts who advocated desegregation.

This wasn't the only thing Anthis did to sabotage racial balance. Board vice president Jeff Towles, an African-American, had voted against "Today and Tomorrow." This was a plan Anthis and the board majority put before voters in the form of a referendum to raise $5 million a year for the FWCS budget. Among other things, it was sold as a way to pay for voluntary transfers of black students to white, suburban schools.

Towles didn't buy it. He thought the racial balance features of the plan were weak and said so repeatedly.

The surgeon paid for his dissent. Anthis conspired with other board members to reject Towles' bid to become the district's first black board president. Here was the surgeon whose great skill had saved civil rights leader Vernon Jordan's life after he was shot in Fort Wayne. Like a naughty schoolboy, Towles had to be "disciplined," Anthis confided to another board member.

Revelations of such mischief had strengthened Rolland's resolve to pursue the cause until the schools were desegregated. But Anthis and the board's treatment of the beloved black surgeon was the last straw for Rolland. Upon hearing Towles' account, he decided to give Taylor and the biracial PQEI group the green light to file a class-action lawsuit. It was done September 13, 1986 in what probably would be the most far-reaching business the U.S. District Court of Northern Indiana would ever undertake.

Chapter Twenty-Six

THE BIG DEAL

It was too cold that morning for my usual jog through Foster Park, near our home. Mostly, I was just antsy to get downtown. At my office, I couldn't concentrate reading the national papers, normally my routine.

As I left the stodgy grey newspaper building on Main Street and headed for the Grile Administration Center, the guard at the door, Tom, an African-American, greeted me for the second time that day, saying something about my going out of the newsroom so early. I said yeah and kept moving. I hurried across Main Street to the parking lot, pulling up my trench coat collar against the biting wind.

The rush hour traffic had thinned, as it does that time in the morning, normalcy crowding in on this pending revolution. I glanced at the familiar scene as I wheeled out of the parking lot, noting old St. Joseph Hospital around the corner. The hospital, in stiff competition from two suburban hospitals, had been a financially troubled institution for years. But it was still treating patients, many of them the parents of the black kids about to have their lives changed forever.

By the time I got to the Grile building, the board room was packed—a sea of familiar faces, administrators, lawyers, advocates, reporters from both daily newspapers and Frost, the black weekly.

I sensed an air of celebration. Anthis seemed to be joking with school attorney Bob Walters, while PQEI attorney Taylor huddled with Lincoln CEO Ian Rolland and two black ministers. I made it a point to greet school officials that I knew felt coerced into agreeing to this settlement. Nevertheless, I thought everyone appreciated that the school district had reached a watershed moment.

Even Superintendent Anthis shook my hand. I detected no hostility. I sure wasn't mad at anybody that day. I just felt a lot of good would come from the agreement and it was time to put the old arguments behind.

The attorneys stepped to the microphones to lay out the particulars. School assignments would be voluntary. The district would use magnet schools to racially balance all elementaries. Those schools would feature special programs and be vigorously marketed to ensure that the district could comply with the racial mix of kids it had agreed to.

The next step would be for both sides to appear before the federal district judge who would oversee the agreement, to be in force through the 1996–1997 school year. Even after that date, the district was committing itself to maintain racially balanced elementary schools.

There was one surprise announcement. Superintendent Anthis would retire at the end of the next school year. I found out that this was his idea, a magnanimous gesture that meant a new superintendent, with no history in the often acrimonious desegregation battle, would implement the plan. Meantime, the school board could make a commitment to racial balance a central test for an educator to replace Anthis.

Months later, the board hired veteran administrator Bill Coats. He was a charming and creative administrator who did see to it that the schools were desegregated. Coats had his squabbles with the newly elected conservatives on the board. But those had nothing to do with racial balance.

Even now, years after the PQEI settlement, I think back to that cold winter day in 1989 when the two sides announced the agreement. I marvel at all that has been accomplished. Ending the racial isolation of kids in the elementary schools not only benefited them. It made us a better city.

The day came almost exactly 20 years after citizens, black and white, began to press in earnest for the death knell of segregation. It was one of those rare funerals where you felt like cheering.

Chapter Twenty-Seven

FOR KENDRA

Racial prejudice is dead.

That was the word from Kendra, grade four, Forest Park Elementary School, Fort Wayne, Indiana.

We were reading a book about Rosa Parks and that's how the subject of racial prejudice came up.

It's been more than a decade since the desegregation settlement. I'm retired from the paper, doing my bit as a volunteer tutor, briefly entering the wondrous world of a 10-year-old where prejudice is something only her elders knew. For Kendra, racial prejudice is ancient history.

Art Linkletter, who hosted TV's "Kids Say the Darndest Things," would have found Kendra's words an astonishing revelation and made some appropriate comment.

All I could manage to utter was a surprised "oh" back to this little African-American girl with the smiling brown eyes and outfits that always matched the beads spaced out in her neatly woven braids.

Don't you know anything, she seemed to be telling me, as she glanced down at the drawings of Rosa Parks sitting in a Birmingham city bus. When I gathered my thoughts, I did share some news of my own with Kendra.

Did she know that just a few years ago, most black fourth graders went to all black schools?

Now she had nothing to say to me. I could tell from the look on her face, though, she had no patience that day for science fiction or ancient history or whatever irrelevant nonsense I was peddling.

How I wished at the moment Bill Anthis could have been seated with us at our reading table under the Black History Month display of Dr. King, Frederick Douglas and Harriet Tubman.

Back when he was superintendent, he worried that disrupting the racial patterns in the lower grades would create a firestorm of opposition from both black and white communities, dividing the city. He might have consulted the kids.

Before me, years later, sat one of the chief beneficiaries of the settlement of the lawsuit black and white parents filed against the school district. And she thinks it's just plain dumb to segregate kids. Does she ever. In fact, she regards having white and black kids together in her classroom as a perfectly normal thing, say, like dumping chocolate syrup on vanilla ice cream.

What nobody would expect Kendra to understand is that she would have been treated differently in an all-black school. I've visited enough segregated schools around the country and in our own city to know that she'd be just one more kid who wasn't reading at grade level. So she wouldn't get the special attention she gets in an integrated school.

Her teachers would expect less than at desegregated Forest Park. In turn, she'd probably expect less of herself. My guess is that nobody in such a school would push her hard to do better. And it would be less likely anyone would notice her learning disability, one of the big things holding her back.

Sometimes I find myself watching the girl closely and wondering what will become of her. She's so cute she can steal your heart without even throwing one of her ever-so-subtle I-know-a-secret smiles your way. Yes, teachers at the school talk of ways to boost her academics and address her learning problems. But she had an unsteady start even before she went to kindergarten.

Moreover, I know that Kendra is dead wrong about racial prejudice. Someday, she'll take her place in a society where many people will judge her according to the color of her skin. I'm saddened by the thought. I know that just reading about Rosa Parks refusing to surrender her seat on a bus won't stiffen Kendra's backbone to stand up to racial slights.

Spunky at times, she's still a sensitive child, quick to pouting, to tears.

Nonetheless, this integrated school has put Kendra far ahead of the game. She studies, eats her hot dogs at lunch and plays kickball with white classmates. She has crossed the color line at an age she is learning that she's a true peer, the equal of every white child.

In turn, her classmates see her not as a racial stereotype but as an individual. For all the hardships she may face, segregation's stigma of inferiority doesn't brand this child. Not now. I pray never.

I guess I shouldn't be surprised that for Kendra, racial prejudice isn't something that happens in her world. Which means she's better prepared to handle those times when she stumbles onto the exceptions.

Chapter Twenty-Eight

IN PRAISE OF LETTERS

Did the Golden Pen Award sell newspapers?

I doubt it.

But the award did make us a better newspaper. And a better community.

When Craig Klugman left his teaching job at Northwestern University in 1982 to become The Journal Gazette's editor, he brought along a bunch of dandy ideas. One was the Golden Pen Award.

Since Craig's early days, the paper has awarded more than 250 gold-colored pens, one every month, to the writer whose letter the editorial board judged the best that month.

Within a few years, publisher Dick Inskeep and Craig established an annual banquet. It's held at a private club to honor the writer who wrote the best letter that year. (We called that award the Golden Pen of the Year, a title that made up in clarity what it lacked in originality.) We made a big deal out of the event, with honored guests and the best fudge sundaes in Indiana for dessert.

We presented the winner with a large, framed copy of the person's letter and ran it as a full page ad in Sunday's paper. We invited prominent people to speak, including Sen. Dick Lugar, Mayor Paul Helmke, Bill Coats, the school superintendent, E.J. Dionne, a Washington Post columnist, Jim Brady, the press secretary shot when John Hinckley tried to assassinate President Reagan, and Miles Brand, the president of Indiana University. (Brand was the guy who fired legendary coach Bob Knight.)

The paper's Golden Pen award gave us more letters to the editor. It created a lot of good will for the paper. It gave a prominence to the voice of the people that it never had before on the editorial pages. The award showed community activists a good way to get their cause before the public.

Above all, by raising the status of letter writers, the award became a tradition in the community, in the best spirit of democracy. Each month, the recognition declared this wonderful ideal America ought to strive for: Everybody's opinion matters. People hesitate to write a letter to the editor. They fear offending somebody. Such as their boss. Or, they fear retaliation from somebody who takes issue with what they wrote. And I've had people promise to write but they never get around to it. These are the people who never get around to sending their aunt in Des Moines a birthday card.

Repercussions were rare. When they did occur, they showed up in the form of somebody else's letter to the editor. Exercising editorial judgment, I wouldn't let somebody make a personal attack on another letter writer. But such letters didn't come in all that often.

I never heard of anybody being fired or even reprimanded at work over a letter that had been published in the newspaper. (Of course, that doesn't mean it didn't happen.)

Seasoned activists had always used the letters column to get their cause before the public. They also made sure I knew they had a letter coming my way.

For many years, Dorothy Frary had been the community's best advocate for the humane treatment of dogs and cats. She engineered the demise of a high-altitude chamber the animal shelter used to kill unwanted pets—a method regarded by experts as needlessly cruel.

Later, as a member of the animal control commission, she championed the creation of a low-cost spay and neuter clinic. No surprise to Dorothy, that clinic helped reduce the population of unwanted pets. The clinic also reduced the number of animals the shelter killed.

When she wanted something in the paper, she would show up at my door, apologize for interrupting and then ask me to read her letter to see if it was all right. No sweat. In fact, her letters were a model of clarity and fairness, starting with the opening sentence that told you what the letter was about.

Likewise, Tom and Jane Dustin, among the most respected environmentalists in the Midwest, would set forth their arguments in letters with grace and boldness but without disparaging those who disagreed with them.

They never complained if we had to trim their copy. When I'd mention that his piece ran a bit long, Tom would reassure me that the cuts didn't bother him, explaining, "Everybody needs an editor."

Besides the letters column, the page opposite the editorial page offers an ideal platform for any citizen advocate. Newspapers have dubbed the page op. ed. The longer format lets the writer develop a case for a cause more fully than in a letter.

I told writers they'd have the best luck if they stuck to what they knew firsthand and, as much as possible, made the writing concrete and personal. Granted, we published a number of pretty good op. ed. pieces that were neither. Whatever the case, I encouraged people to talk to me about what they planned to write. For my own reasons as well as the writer's, I wanted the column to sing.

If people hesitate to write letters or op. ed. pieces, for some reason many also hesitate to contact an editor, reporter or feature writer to get somebody at the paper to write something. Those who've learned to make a contact often are surprised at how welcomed they are.

We hosted editorial board meetings for advocates of every imaginable cause. Or an editorial writer would meet with them. If the advocates made a decent case, we'd be persuaded to their point of view and take up their cause. The route of a new superhighway in the state, saving an old train station, and protecting precious park land from the encroachment of a parking lot for the children's zoo were just a few examples of how advocates enlisted the newspaper.

I encouraged people with a story or editorial idea to first contact the editorial writer, reporter or feature writer. Here's why: It's the writer who most needs to buy into your idea if the piece is to be as effective as possible. If the topic is assigned by an editor, the writer might not show the same enthusiasm. Or, it could get a low priority on the writer's list of assignments.

Now if somebody asked me about where to direct a news release, I told them to send a separate one each to editors, reporters and editorial writers. (You might reasonably assume people in a newsroom would share hot issues with each other. Sorry.)

But for all the openings our paper gave readers to promote their ideas, I put letters to the editor at the top of the list. Only the front page and the obituaries attract more readers. To the chagrin of us Big Thinks, the newspaper's editorials lagged far behind them all.

Only with a letter to the editor are you assured as broad a readership, from civic leaders to the butcher and the homemaker.

In a brief space, you get to educate and maybe even inspire hundreds if not thousands of readers.

Just remember, your letter to the editor has a swell chance of getting published. Not a bad deal for doing a lot of good.

Chapter Twenty-Nine

UP IN SMOKE

They were my very own gang of four.

That's what I called them. These city council members had launched a revolution to overthrow the established order.

Indeed, few things we've done in Fort Wayne have changed the daily lives of more people than the ban on smoking in restaurants.

That ban truly was a revolution. We owed its success to these four, pro-business conservatives on the council. No more is it a smoker's prerogative to blow smoke in other people's faces in city restaurants.

I served as the council members' noisiest cheerleader.

They came to see me in the newsroom office one afternoon, all dressed up as if for a job interview, as they prepared to introduce their ordinances. One would ban smoking in the workplace, the second would ban smoking in restaurants.

Needless to say, restaurant owners and smokers took exception. It was early summer in 1998. I had written so many editorials calling for a ban on smoking in restaurants I probably deserved to be on some smoker's hit list.

Back in the 80s, I wrote to support an ordinance that required restaurants to provide a non-smoking area. Of course, as any non-smoker can tell you, such restrictions can be so weak you can be seated at a non-smoking table just a few inches from a table for smokers. Who'll take your complaint?

Naturally, like all former smokers, I got accused of having the zeal of a convert to a new religion, the ultimate put-down in that context. Well, probably closer to the mark, I knew I had polluted the air of my two kids for years and blamed myself for their recurrent respiratory ailments as adults.

After I quit smoking—it took gall bladder surgery to force me to break the habit—I discovered the curse of second-hand smoke. Are former smokers more sensitive to cigarette smoke than those who never smoked? I don't know. I do know that after I quit, the smell of cigarettes drove me crazy.

Moreover, as I researched the subject, I learned that second-hand smoke can cause heart problems, ear infections in children, and trigger attacks for people who suffer from asthma. I learned inhaling second-hand smoke regularly can give you cancer.

When they showed up in the newsroom, the four council members knew full well they would get the paper's support for a ban on smoking in restaurants. After all, we had backed the valiant if unsuccessful fight of former councilman, attorney Mark GiaQuinta for a strict ban years before.

But I was glad they had come to reassure me that they were in the fight to stay, and to win. (I could be as critical in editorials of people who abandoned good causes as of those who opposed them.)

As they talked and I listened, I was dismayed that they had yet to enlist prominent civic leaders, particularly Lincoln National CEO Ian Rolland, whose column on banning smoking at his company ran as a Newsweek "My Turn."

This go-around would be different. Two physicians sat on the council. Republican Dr. John Crawford treated cancer patients, and Democrat Dr. Tom Hayhurst specialized in respiratory diseases.

Moreover, both men came across as fair-minded and reasonable. They were courteous toward those who appeared before the council to object to their proposals. They looked for ways to strike compromises with those who disagree with them.

Republican council President Rebecca Ravine, a business consultant, joined the docs. An outgoing person, with enough charm to make up for her male colleagues' sober countenances, she often called me to talk strategy.

Veteran Councilman Don Schmidt was the third Republican in the group. Over the years, Don—maybe the most conservative of all on the council—and I had engaged in a lot of arguments. But on this subject, we were of one accord. A professor of engineering at Indiana University-Purdue University Fort Wayne, he held the record on the council for having fought for such an ordinance the longest, more than a decade.

The four's big challenge was to win another vote to get a majority and pass the ordinance to ban smoking in restaurants. That wouldn't be easy. They weren't worried about winning support for a ban on smoking in the workplace. (Employers at most businesses and companies had already banned workplace smoking voluntarily; retail stores and the shopping malls had followed suit.) Restaurants were another matter.

While all council members said they knew that second-hand smoke could cause health problems, you heard a lot of arguments from several about not wanting to interfere in somebody's business.

I thought Dr. Crawford did a great job answering this. In one letter to the editor, he pointed out his conservative, pro-business history and philosophy but argued that the public health came first.

Other objections surfaced. Democrat Tom Henry had a family member in the restaurant business. He argued the council should be sensitive toward the owners, not forcing something on them at the expense of new construction.

(The ordinance wouldn't ban all smoking. It only required that the restaurant separate smokers from non-smokers. In practice, though, few eateries would go to the expense of creating a separate room for the smokers.)

Republican Dede Hall, married to one of the brothers who ran a chain of seven family restaurants, objected that bars and private clubs had been exempted from the ordinance.

"It's just not fair," she kept insisting during one discussion around the council table. She was right. But if the council tacked on bars and private clubs to the regulation, it would have invited far more opposition, probably killing the proposed ordinance.

I thought Hall should not vote on the ordinance that dealt with restaurants, as that would have been a conflict of interest. I put that opinion in an editorial. Hall ignored the opinion and acted as if she didn't see me when I ran into her at Kroger's.

I never had a good handle on why the two African-Americans on the council, Democrats Cletis Edmonds and Archie Lunsey, tried to duck the public controversy. As a rule, our black councilmen would back any ordinance that even sounded progressive. But Edmonds predicted customer preferences eventually would force the restaurants to go non-smoking. The ordinance wouldn't be needed. Lunsey nodded, I assumed in agreement.

The Republican police officer on the council, Marty Bender, said he'd vote to ban smoking in the workplace, but he felt that restaurants were different: Nobody forced you to eat in a restaurant that allowed smoking.

From the standpoint of the editorial page, the controversy, which dragged on for months, generated lots of letters. I printed all of them except those that accused the four council members of being Nazis. That was a bit much.

To their credit, council members debated their points with courtesy. That marked a big change from the shouting matches that erupted during council meetings 20 years before.

The decorum wasn't all that had changed. During council meetings of former days, council President Vivian Schmidt could be seen holding a cigarette. The bearded Councilman Ben Eisbart might be puffing on his pipe, while former Mayor Mike Burns fingered the stub of a smelly cigar.

During the 1998 debate on the smoking ordinance, featuring a mostly new cast of characters, no council member smoked. Nor did anyone in the audience. By this time, smoking had been banned in public buildings, in the city and county. Curiously, no council member objected to this rule. Nor, as far as I knew, did any restaurant owner.

I've always been a fan of public hearings. They can be terrific forums in which the public can educate and lobby their elected officials. Yes, they can be tedious. If the chairperson fails to set time limits, some citizens are bound to filibuster. The public hearing on the smoking ordinances proved a happy exception.

People got three minutes to speak. Chairman John Crawford also announced several names of speakers at a time. That way, no time would be wasted as citizens found their way to the microphone.

It turned out to be a fascinating, enlightening and even inspiring parade of citizens. People from the advocacy groups served up the facts. Dr. Frank Byrne, a lung specialist, stepped forward to explain why all three of the city's hospitals had banned smoking. He cited the "extensive scientific" evidence that found even limited exposure to second-hand smoke can represent a serious health risk.

The woman who owned Cindy's Diner, something of a landmark downtown, testified that when her restaurant went non-smoking, business actually picked up.

Council members became especially attentive when a man with asthma explained that he couldn't remember when he had eaten at a restaurant. He avoided restaurants because he didn't want to risk an asthma attack.

Darlene Amstutz of Smokefree Indiana reported on that group's informal survey of several hundred homes in the city. According to that survey, the vast majority of residents supported the ban on smoking in restaurants.

Dr. Crawford read a written statement from the Chamber of Commerce. The business group announced that it would remain neutral on both ordinances. That was a terrific victory for my four council revolutionaries. Normally, just as you could count on the sun to rise each day, you could rely on the chamber to oppose any regulation that the city council discusses that might, by any stretch of the imagination, cost any of its members profit.

Chamber officials and many business leaders must have choked on the neutrality decision.

I had a good hunch how that came about. I guessed that the council members pushing the smoking ordinances hadn't made the contact with Lincoln National's Rolland. So I took it on myself to call him. Indeed, no council member had been in touch.

I reminded Rolland that he had led Lincoln to be the first major corporation in the city to go non-smoking. So would he lean on the chamber not to oppose the legislation?

A few days later, he called to say he had met with the chamber's executive committee. I didn't have to ask what his argument was. A Fort Wayne native, he worried more about the city's reputation. He insisted that the city be known as a progressive leader in the country, just as it had after the desegregation settlement. He guessed, given the reception the committee gave him, the chamber would remain neutral.

Both bills restricting smoking passed. The vote was overwhelming for the ban on workplace smoking. But council President Ravine and her cohorts only picked up one extra vote to restrict smoking in restaurants. That was the city police officer, Marty Bender. I worried that Republican Mayor Paul Helmke would sign the measure regarding the workplace but might veto the ordinance restricting smoking in restaurants. A few days after council's vote, I got my chance to sound him out.

Deputy Editorial Page Editor Evan Davis and I bumped into Helmke on the street over the lunch hour. We were heading for the Three Rivers Festival in progress in the new downtown park along the river. I asked the mayor if he planned to sign the smoking ordinances. Well, he explained, he sure wasn't in favor of smoking. But he'd have to study the bills further—this from a lawyer who doubtless had followed the council debates—and he did worry about interfering with business.

He signed the ordinance that applied to the workplace. The son-of-a-gun then vetoed the bill that pertained to restaurants.

At this point, it was hard to imagine how my gang of four could pick up a sixth vote needed to override the mayor's veto. In dealing with all these people, I had concluded that Edmonds simply wouldn't change his vote. Lunsey was another matter. Once, this inner-city African-American had run as a Republican. Now, as a Democrat, just as before, he didn't seem to hold fixed positions. I telephoned him.

A few days later, he stood outside my office. He'd been thinking about what I had told him earlier. Yes, he said, he respected the restaurant owners' position, and knew that patrons, after all, could exercise a choice. But he'd been out a night or two before with his family to a restaurant. They were seated near smokers, and at each table, children sat with their parents. It dawned on him that those young ones, among the most at risk from second-hand smoke, had no choice. (I had pointed out this rather obvious fact to all the council members earlier.)

I escorted him into the newsroom so he could tell his story to a reporter. He would vote to override the mayor's veto. The ban on smoking in restaurants picked up that critical sixth vote and would become city law. But to my great regret, the editorials failed to persuade the county to follow suit.

If the county had also banned smoking in restaurants, that would have undercut the argument of the restaurant owners in the city that their patrons would take their business to eateries in the country.

Even for the city, the controversy had another act before the final curtain.

Councilwoman Dede Hall's family filed lawsuits in federal and state courts to overturn the ordinance that applied to res-taurants. Those court battles stretched out for months. But in the meantime, the fire department did send inspectors to see that the restaurants were obeying the new law and to fine those that weren't.

Eventually, the lawsuits failed. Fort Wayne now has the toughest restriction on smoking in restaurants of any Indiana city.

This revolution on behalf of the public health had prevailed. Most opponents of the ban have long since forgiven me. Needless to say, we're all breathing easier.

Chapter Thirty

HARMLESS AS DOVES

"Can two walk together except they be agreed?" That's the prophet Amos. The answer is that it depends.

The smoking ban was a good example of how I worked with people that I had disagreed with on other issues. That's in the best tradition of social reform.

Whether somebody was a liberal or conservative, I searched for common ground. Often, I thought we were so far apart, I was surprised when I did find a basis for working together.

In the case of the ordinance on smoking, it was the public health, particularly that of children. In the battle to desegregate the elementary schools, for some people it was compliance with the law of the land and, for others, it was the city's image as a progressive community.

I had to accept a result that was less than perfect. For example, I didn't want separate dining rooms for smokers. The ordinance allows that. Yet it's worked out. In practice, most restaurants didn't go to the trouble to create the physically separated smoking room.

At first, I didn't want the desegregation settlement to use voluntary means to racially balance the elementaries. I doubted that a voluntary plan would get the job done. I was wrong. The settlement created magnet schools, which let parents choose. That's worked out, too.

I can't think of one reform our editorials endorsed that didn't require us to cross ideological lines. When I think of a legislator who spoke up for a bill to separate juvenile offenders from adults, I think of the county's former Republican Sheriff Bud Meeks. I was on hand during a senate committee hearing when this state senator made a passionate appeal on behalf of these kids.

Bud and I had lots of arguments through the years. A few years after the committee hearing, he joined other Republican lawmakers who vehemently objected to a drama student's production of "Corpus Christi" at Indiana University-Purdue University Fort Wayne. The play depicts Jesus and his disciples as homosexual.

I didn't think that as a student project the production was worth all the fuss. But rather than argue with him, I just listened to Bud's complaint as we stood among the stacks at the downtown library, following a meeting on plans for a high-speed train through the city.

"Always make a good case for the other side," my old philosophy professor, T.G. Burks, used to say.

That's great advice. If you make the other guy's case, you're forced to do more research so you can answer him. Better than that, making his case forces you to listen to the other side with an open mind. With that attitude, you can afford to get off your high horse and show some humility.

I don't know if this is the kind of thing Jesus had in mind when he said the meek shall inherit the earth. But the meek sure can make great activists. They change the world. Examples? How about Gandhi or the Buddha? Or Jesus?

Getting stuck in an ideology is a killer. Sure, you can make a lot of noise. You can even lead a big march on Washington such as those my wife and I witnessed the year we lived in the nation's capital. But you probably won't move matters off the dime and change the status quo.

First, you've oversimplified life, the world and practically everything that's in it. Second, you wear people out with your tirades. Third, you're a bore. Worst of all, you've lost your chance of helping somebody else break free from his mindset.

Shunning ideology doesn't mean you can't show passion. It came naturally to me on some issues, such as racial prejudice, the mistreatment of kids, the death penalty. You can easily overdo passion, though. Sometimes, I even surprised myself that I hadn't alienated a mayor, senator or judge with my intensity (which a friend, the Rev. Dr. Dick Hamm, once pointed out could sound hostile). I guess it proved how tolerant people can be with somebody on a mission.

It's far better to show a genuine interest in the person you're trying to win over. That can keep a friendship even if you haven't won a convert.

At a Harborfront seafood restaurant in Baltimore during a conference, eight members of the Education Writers Association gathered at a table near the door, overlooking the brick-lined promenade and, beyond that, lights playing off the water in the harbor.

I sat next to Jim Bencivenga, the former education editor of the Christian Science Monitor. At that time, Jim was a spokesman for the U.S. Department of Education under President Reagan.

Despite that we had been friends, we got into a devil of an argument, the subject of which I can't remember. What does stick is how, quite by accident, I managed to extricate us from this argument neither of us was going to win. I recall that he made some reference to his college days, and I jumped in right away and asked him about where he grew up, his parents and so forth.

Within seconds, the tone of the conversation changed. His countenance changed. He no longer looked angry and about ready to smack me. He smiled and his voice softened. I'm sure I changed in like fashion.

What could be more important for the activist than to learn how to deal with other people?

"Be wise as serpents, as harmless as doves," Jesus admonished his disciples.

"A soft answer turns away wrath," the book of Proverbs reminds us.

In our heart of hearts, we know the wisdom of these ancient sayings. We can observe their power in others. But you make adopting such a philosophy of human relations all the harder if you believe only your side has the truth or the right answer and you treat the other side as a bunch of fools.

Martin Luther King, Jr. preached a great deal about loving one's enemies. That included bystanders who spat upon civil rights marchers. It included the police who turned dogs and fire hoses on those who were only demanding that the promise of freedom and democracy be theirs.

King and other civil rights leaders trained thousands of advocates in the tactics of non-violence and taught them ways to accept the taunts and the blows of the billy clubs without complaining, without retaliating. Such self-restraint is the crucial discipline of the activist. It's as important as staying focused on your goal, as important as sticking with your cause even when it seems hopeless.

I tried not to demonize those who disagreed with me or to assume they simply would never listen to reason. That's the sure way to become cynical. Then you're of little use as an activist.

A more honest, more realistic attitude for the activist to adopt is this: Sometimes, the most bullheaded, self-righteous person can come to see things in a different light—in a word, to change. The activist's willingness to care about that person, to be a true friend, can make that change happen.

You won't have lost a solitary thing.

Chapter Thirty-One

MAIN STREET PEACENIKS

It must sound nuts today, now more than 20 years after the city council's debate, more than a decade after the fall of the Soviet Union. But for a couple of weeks in Fort Wayne ending the nuclear arms race between the superpowers moved to the top of the issue heap.

I still scratch my head in wonderment that a group of people so often preoccupied with unadulterated silliness took on something so monumental as the arms race.

I know part of the answer. If you get the City Clerk to dust off the video of the council's meetings from late 1981, you would see that council members took their deliberations over the nuclear freeze resolution as seriously as any discussion about a raise for police officers and firefighters or a tax abatement for a new business.

I took a particular interest in the debate. That was because it was my idea. I had coaxed Council President Vivian Schmidt into introducing the resolution. First, I have to backtrack.

Earlier in the fall, Ken Brown, director of nearby Manchester College's peace studies program, and I took a few of his students to New York City for a peace conference at historic Riverside Church in Harlem. The ride in Ken's old VW van was itself a religious experience, as our faith in one another's humanity got put to the severest test.

Once at that famous church in New York, I was transported into realms beyond the daily humdrum of knocking out editorials and playing cribbage with my kids. Indeed, it gave me chills, this former theological student, to sit in the sanctuary of the church where Harry Emerson Fosdick thundered against the powers that be of his day.

Now, at the time of this peace conference, Yale's famous anti-war chaplain, the Reverend William Sloane Coffin, was serving as the church's senior minister. What a sermon, worthy of Fosdick, he unloaded that Sunday morning on this motley collection of veteran peaceniks and would-be anti-nuclear activists. It reminded me of Old Testament prophets like Isaiah and Amos and Jeremiah.

After a few days among these folk, listening to Coffin and other heroes of the peace movement, I knew exactly what I had to do when I got back to Fort Wayne.

Other cities, mainline Protestant churches, and advocacy groups already had called on the United States and the Soviet Union to end development and deployment of nuclear weapons. They called it the nuclear freeze movement.

I sensed an opportunity had presented itself for communities across the country to have an impact on national defense policy and, possibly, change the course of history. Fort Wayne, I humbly decided, should take the lead in Indiana.

I wrote editorials to remind readers how both the Soviets and the United States had enough nuclear weapons to destroy each other's cities many times over. I pointed out that the destruction would cause death on a scale that had no precedent in human history. I noted that disaster planning would be pointless.

After all, what kind of defense could possibly be conceived to protect the American population from the devastation of weapons with 2,000 times the force of the bomb that we dropped on Hiroshima?

I didn't stop with editorials. Privately, I urged friends to write letters to the editor supporting a nuclear freeze resolution. I called members of the clergy. Perhaps the most important one in those years was Fort Wayne-South Bend Catholic Diocese Bishop Bill McManus.

Despite our theological differences—I supported abortion rights which he of course opposed—McManus and I had become good friends. I could count on him to dash off an op. ed. piece, even if it took issue with my editorial. He had desegregated Chicago's Catholic schools back when he was that district's superintendent. That alone made me a fan. On issues of war and peace, I knew exactly where he stood. With me and the rest of the angels.

Sure, he said, he'd be glad to contact council members and

urge them to support the freeze resolution. With his support, I was confident the resolution would prevail. Naturally, council members, being the showboats they were, let their debate get pretty heated. At one point, the city clerk himself, Charlie Westerman, jumped in. An old pol, he knew the council members only too well. So when former Mayor Mike Burns showed no interest in a handout one of the freeze advocates passed out, Charlie demanded that he read it. It was so like Burns to blow off some fact that didn't agree with his opinion. He had made his pronouncements on the resolution without bothering to read what the freeze advocate had submitted. "Only a fool," he declared in his customary tone of certitude, "would try to tell the president what to do while he's in delicate negotiations with the Russians."

"No, Mike. In a democracy we are all responsible."

That was Sam Talarico correcting his curmudgeonly colleague. As a rule, Sam said very little during council debates. But here, calmly rebuking Burns with a few words, Talarico showed why it was a city council's business to take a position on the nuclear arms race.

Councilman John Nuckols, chairing the meeting, put his view of the matter at hand in the most personal terms:

"I want to stay here [*in the world*] as long as I can," he said, dark brown eyes darting around the table as if to dare anyone to propose any policy that might shorten his life.

Several times, Council President Schmidt pointed out that the resolution didn't ask the United States to destroy its nuclear weapons, only not to make more of them.

When it was all said and done, the council adopted the freeze resolution. Six council members voted for it. One voted against. Two, including Burns, abstained.

In the great scheme of things the Fort Wayne City Council's vote on the nuclear freeze resolution didn't amount to much. But when that vote got tallied with the hundreds of others in communities around the country, the exercise accomplished something important.

Just a few years later, President Reagan met with Soviet President Mikhail Gorbachev in Reykjavik, Iceland. Going well beyond anything the freeze movement people imagined, the two agreed to scrap all nuclear weapons.

Of course, before they boarded their planes to head for home, their staffs got to the two superpower leaders and persuaded them to wise up. The deal was off. Nevertheless, the nuclear arms race did slow to an unenthusiastic trot.

Moreover, the national debate, echoed in our own city council, provided an education for the public on nuclear weapons. That was badly in need of updating. In less than a half century, the bombs used against Japan in 1945 had become obsolete. By the end of the Cold War, the United States and the Soviet Union were armed with thousands of hydrogen weapons, each one many times more horrific than the bombs dropped on Hiroshima and Nagasaki.

Clearly, the day had come when Americans could no longer plausibly believe that they could protect themselves in a nuclear war.

With that bit of education accomplished, Mike Burns and the rest of them could go back to worrying about the escalating cost of fixing potholes.

Chapter Thirty-Two

GUN STORY

"You got creamed."

I could have lived happily ever after if the woman hadn't told me about how lousy I had been on the TV show.

Let's put it this way. It wasn't my finest hour.

By the time of my appearance on the "Dick Wolfsie Show," I was a veteran in the gun control wars. Surely, no other daily newspaper in Indiana could match our passion for tough regulation of handguns.

But that day I got a painful reminder that passion isn't everything. Nor are facts.

And I'd get that reminder on a popular TV talk show. It was broadcast before a live audience from the renovated Union Station in downtown Indianapolis.

I prepared thoroughly. After all, another guest on the show was none other than Don Davis, the Midwest's biggest gun dealer and best known for his TV commercials where he proclaimed, "I just love to sell guns."

I knew I could count on Don to produce all the arguments of why everybody should own a gun. For my part, I had memorized more than 100 facts, backed by research, to prove why carrying or having a gun around the house made you less safe.

A friend at Handgun Control, Inc., in Washington, D.C., coached me on how to handle this gun dealer. She advised me not to look at him and pretend he wasn't there. (Dumb idea; on the video I looked aloof, disengaged, rude.)

Don, of course, was a master salesman. He had lots of practice being on television. From the start to the end of the program, he befriended me. Ruddy-faced, with thick greying hair and a white mustache, he was my pal. He treated me as a poor, misguided fellow who just needed to hear his stories.

He told how he had saved his own life when he flashed his gun as some black fellow approached him at an ATM machine.

Was the guy arrested?

No, he had scared him off.

Don produced a lengthy news article on the rise in violence. I pointed out that the article proved nothing about the wisdom of keeping a gun for protection.

But early on, I sensed I wasn't winning over the studio audience. Later I viewed the videotape. My thorough preparation came across well, though I sounded stuffy and condescending—not to mention windy—as I tried to cram all my 100 facts into my responses to Don.

I hadn't counted on the power of Don's common-sense arguments. Nor had I realized how the fear of violent crime would manifest itself in the minds of the studio audience. You couldn't blame the climate of fear only on the gun dealers like Don or the NRA and its gun-toting actor and defender Charlton Heston. Daily newspapers like my own did their bit, too, by highlighting stories of violent crime.

As the debate progressed, it became crystal clear that audience wasn't buying my argument that carrying a handgun or keeping one at your bedside made you less, not more, safe.

But what does it take? If hearing about years of research doesn't help people see the light, how do they ever get the picture? I'm thinking such things as the talk show continues. (Oh, I could be so smug.)

Maybe if people could sit in the pew of a black church during a funeral of some 16-year-old kid shot dead by some other kid, often younger, they would grasp the real menace of guns.

Speaking for myself, I could hardly bear the anguish and the anger as I would leave an inner-city church after a service that could go on for a couple of hours. It was useless to fight back the tears. I never could imagine how family and friends of the boy could bear the pain.

Unfortunately, lots of people had attended the same funerals I had. Yet some of them still believed keeping a gun around protected them. Even when a young victim had himself been packing a gun, people didn't connect the dots.

As for those in suburbs, where gun violence is rare, the weapons still seemed to be everywhere, a talisman that was supposed to keep the bad guys at bay. People in such neighborhoods also had funerals of gun victims to attend.

There, it wasn't the funeral of a kid who didn't pay off his drug dealer on time. It was the funeral of a mere child who didn't know Dad's gun was loaded. It was the funeral of some poor depressed soul who had to pick just about the most lethal weapon he could find around the house to take his own life.

Looking back, I suppose I could have tried to portray Don as just a buffoon who spoke only out of financial self-interest, a hawker and huckster of death. Indeed, his cornball style made him a tempting target to mock.

I did work in the point that the biggest supplier of guns to the bad guys is dealers like Don. I noticed a guy in the audience smirk at my sarcasm. Months later, thieves made my point for me.

They broke into Don's big Indianapolis store and hauled off enough guns to start a war. You could be sure these guns didn't end up in the purses of nice little old ladies.

When it came time for questions, a couple of women in the audience stood to agree with Don and rebut my argument about the risks of keeping guns around.

One lady said she carried a gun. Women sitting nearby nodded their heads in approval. I asked her if some mugger held a gun on her how she was supposed to get her gun out of her purse before the guy shot her. She just glared at me and sat down in a huff, shaking her head as if I were just too plain dumb to understand.

My task of enlightening a few folks seemed hopeless. But the ordeal gave me a powerful lesson that I often failed to appreciate. People weigh somebody else's "facts" against their own experience and values. Even the heartbreak of a child's funeral won't necessarily end a person's defense of guns for protection.

But when facts and science won't do it, sometimes a personal experience can turn somebody's head completely around. We all know about some guy who never wears a seat belt. That is, until he gets banged up in a car accident. Then, he becomes the town's great apostle of seat belts.

Likewise, I've also seen how people with no strong feelings on guns can have a routine encounter that crystallizes their thinking and they became an advocate for gun control. That happened for our publisher, Dick Inskeep, a longtime hunter who never said much one way or the other about our gun control editorials.

I recall one meeting of our editorial board. The night before, Dick had been at the Memorial Coliseum for the annual gun show. He attended lots of events at this huge arena, having served for years on the board.

The building, on the city's north side, hosts rock concerts, Fort Wayne Komet hockey games, home and garden shows and gun shows. But Dick rarely made a comment about an event at the Coliseum. That day was the exception.

He told how as he walked past booths displaying a variety of firearms, he noticed young kids fondling large, semi-automatic handguns. It made him uncomfortable. Two things struck him. First was how fascinated the kids were with the guns. Second was how easy it would be for them to acquire such guns. Dick connected the dots.

Not long before that editorial board meeting, the teenage son of a prominent black minister, the Reverend Ternae Jordan, had been shot in the head as he sat in the lobby of the neighborhood YMCA waiting for a family member to pick him up. Presumably, it was another inner-city kid who fired the shot.

Thank goodness, the boy survived. But the near tragedy made an impression on people throughout the city, beyond the black community. That included my publisher. Dick not only knew the family, his wife Harriet sat on a foundation board with Rev. Jordan. Meantime, the minister started his own anti-gun violence crusade with his "Stop the Madness" campaign.

At the editorial board meeting that day, somebody asked Dick what he proposed we say about guns. He looked straight at me, with an expression as serious as I had ever seen, and told me to call for a ban on the sale of handguns.

They should only be for the police, he added.

Naturally, I complied. I developed that theme in the editorial for the next day and in subsequent editorials. I rarely got such a vivid green light from Dick on most other radical ideas. As a rule, however, the editorials only drew angry rebuttals from local members of the National Rifle Association.

Later, I was delighted when two members of the city council, Tom Henry and Charles Redd, proposed that the city register handguns. The Chicago suburb of Morton Grove, Illinois, had banned them. Other communities, by the mid-1980s, also were taking up the issue. But like my editorials calling for gun control, the councilmen's proposal drew mostly the wrath of the NRA folks. The resolution was quietly tabled. And forgotten.

But I've always been thankful for small victories. Because

I nagged the people at Handgun Control, Inc., so often, they got to know me. Sarah Brady led the group and making that connection helped a lot when I was urging Congress to pass the so-called Brady bill, named after Jim Brady.

Although our politics diverge, Jim remains a hero to me. Shot when John Hinckley was trying to assassinate President Reagan, Jim bravely endures the pain and disability he suffers from that near tragedy. But I also regard him a hero for becoming such an eloquent spokesman for gun control.

I invited Jim to come to Fort Wayne to speak at the paper's annual Golden Pen Awards Banquet, held to recognize letter writers whose work had been selected as the letter of the month over the past year. What a personal honor to introduce Jim.

The theme of his speech couldn't have been more appropriate. Lauding the letter writers, he cited their example to show how important it is for every citizen to get involved in public policy.

If ordinary citizens were as vocal as members of the NRA, the country would have sensible gun control by now. Certainly, the Brady Law, named in Jim's honor and requiring an instant background check on handgun sales, is a welcome step. But most of us haven't raised the alarm about the merchants of death such as Don Davis. His business doesn't offer protection for most of the public. It remains a menace.

In 2003, using government data, the Brady Campaign to Prevent Gun Violence released a study that found between 1989 and 1996, Davis' gun shop sold 398 guns that were later used in crimes. I could have guessed as much during our debate. I only wish I had emphasized Don's contribution to more gun violence in that TV show, rather than ticking off a bunch of statistics.

When I stop to reflect, I realize gun control is not a hopeless cause. But reform on this issue will take more than editorials and debaters more charming and clever than I. Stirring the public conscience, enlisting community leaders, can be daunting.

In the early 1990s, the National Cathedral in Washington, D.C., held a forum on gun violence. The program featured respected Americans, including Associate Supreme Court Justice Sandra Day O'Connor and former Democratic congressman, the Reverend Robert Drinan. Drinan appealed to the churches to take the lead on gun control. His remarks were so eloquent, he brought the congregation to their feet.

Watching that on TV gave me the idea to challenge the Fort Wayne clergy to take the following Sunday to preach on the perils of the gun culture. I telephoned a half dozen clergymen I knew and brought up the question. I stuck my proposal in an editorial. Most of these religious leaders expressed an interest, though they were noncommittal. Father Tom O'Connor, a priest of an inner-city parish and a guy as good as gold, told me the problem wasn't just guns, it was a lack of jobs.

Monday, I didn't hear from a soul about any sermons on gun control. I guessed there weren't many. Preachers feel at liberty to denounce sins in the abstract. But few will take on their congregations' exaggerated fear of crime or chastise any contributors in the audience who happen to be members of the NRA.

In our community, a metropolitan area of a quarter million people, guns can still claim more than 40 lives every year. That counts homicides, suicides and accidents. Once in a blue moon somebody does save his own life with a gun. But total up the innocent lives lost and you have an avoidable tragedy that touches hundreds of people, many of them children.

Believing the Second Amendment says it's our right, we have armed ourselves with more than 200 million firearms, mostly for protection, almost a gun for every man, woman and child.

Yet we're told we're still not safe. Among many others, Don Davis has seen to that.

Chapter Thirty-Three

JOE'S FATAL FLAW

Two things got me going over the Joe Corcoran case.

One was the jury's recommendation that he be executed for shooting his brother Jim and three other young men at his sister's home on Fort Wayne's north side. They were just four innocent guys in their 30s, watching a ball game and having a beer.

Still, I felt that executing Joe was a big mistake.

I figured Judge Fran Gull, a former prosecutor, would go along with the jury. That would mean this young guy, only 24, would end up on death row at state prison in Michigan City.

The second was what I saw as the failure of the judge, prosecutor and defense attorneys to appreciate the nature of Joe's illness.

Right from the start, people got a glimpse at that when Joe told police detectives he killed these guys because he thought they were talking about him. He surely was mentally ill, and I argued in editorials that since we don't execute the retarded or children in Indiana, we couldn't justify executing somebody as psychotic as Joe.

I got a chance to take the measure of Joe's illness in the Allen County jail, a few weeks after the trial and before the sentencing.

The handsome, dark-haired young man of the news pictures had transformed himself into a portrait of a heartless criminal on a wanted poster. Hair cut down to the nub, face without expression, eyes vacant, Joe mostly talked about his sleep disorder. I noted that for Joe the disorder was a lot more than an annoyance. It had become an obsession.

I had doubts about a psychologist's earlier diagnosis: a personality disorder. It seemed obvious that Joe suffered from something a lot more disabling than a personality disorder. The way he described his sleep disorder sounded more like a paranoid delusion to me. I shared my observation with John Nimmo, the defense attorney, as we walked out of the jail and into the glare of the midsummer sun.

Joe had made the headlines even before these killings in July, 1997. When he was 16, in 1992, the Steuben County prosecutor charged him with shooting his parents to death at their northeast Indiana lake home.

"I really fucked up this time," Joe told the minister who had come to visit him in the county jail.

At the time, the statement came the closest of anything he said to admitting to those killings. As the minister related it to me, years later, the boy said it without much emotion.

You would have thought they stuck him in jail for rear-ending the sheriff's squad car with the family pickup.

A jury acquitted him. To be sure, he had talked to his classmates of wanting to kill his parents. But no physical evidence connected Joe to this crime. Like his dad, though, the boy knew guns. His mother bought him his first when he was 14. The house held a regular arsenal. Joe knew how to clean guns and how to hide the one used in the killings.

Besides, everybody noted how calm he was when he got on the school bus the morning his parents were killed. But somebody with a mental illness can act pretty disconnected to something he's done to harm another person. Counselors see such dissociation in patients all the time.

Unfortunately, the full picture of Joe's illness wouldn't come into focus until after he confessed to the murders at his sister Kelly's home.

I visited with her and her twin sister Kim at that white-frame home in a quiet working-class neighborhood where Joe had shot the four men. These young women, fraternal twins, talked freely of the horrors that had twice intruded into their lives. Kim had discovered her parents' bodies, her mother with a huge hole in her neck, her father's head blown off.

Kelly had been at the store during the second killings and returned home to find Joe acting strangely outside the home and bodies inside. I was amazed that she wanted to continue living in the home. Her insurance had paid for cleaning up the blood, a renovation and new furniture.

Still, I thought the memory of entering the house to find her brother Jim, her fiancé Scott Turner, Doug Stillwell and Tim Bricker staring lifelessly in her living room would haunt her every time she opened the front door. She casually dismissed the question, explaining that nobody had wanted to harm her.

I had seen the videotaped confession and could easily imagine Joe ordering his niece, Kelly's daughter, into her mother's room, then loading an assault rifle from his collection, stepping purposely down the stairs to the landing where he opened fire without saying a word.

At first, Kelly wanted Joe to get the death penalty and told the police that. But eventually she came around to Kim's view that the family didn't need one more death and Joe's execution wouldn't bring anybody back. Both sisters were beginning to grasp the full import of what their older brother Jim had told them many times: "There's something wrong with Joe."

Their father "Corky" had served in the Marines and still liked to wear his combat boots. He was a big fan of Tom Clancy novels. A letter writer to the paper who had worked with Corky described him as a hard worker but a real gung-ho male who would have been a tough disciplinarian with his kids.

The sisters confirmed this characterization to me.

Clearly the mother, Katherine, was a troubled person. Reading her neatly written journals you enter the soul of a sad, worried and guilt-filled woman. She battled her fears and sadness with a fanatical attention to exercise.

Further, she tormented herself with a belief that she was unworthy of God's love. She tried to make amends for whatever sins she imagined by attending her church for prayer meetings and Bible study, as well as Sunday services. Her daughters described her as emotionally aloof. Meantime, she hovered obsessively over Joe, took him to her church programs and lectured him on sticking to the straight and narrow—avoiding what she regarded as the wild ways of his older siblings.

Kelly and Kim related a number of things that might have alerted the family to Joe's unfolding mental illness. At six, he rigged an alarm on his bedroom door to warn him of intruders—which only could have been other family members. As a teenager, he pointed a gun at a friend's father who had scolded him for shooting at stray cats. He shot out a transformer at the power company's installation.

After his parents' deaths, when he worked at the machine shop with Kelly, he started to choke her when she told him he wasn't performing a task correctly. Then there was the obsession with guns.

Despite the girls' suspicion Joe had murdered their parents, Kelly hadn't minded that he kept his father's arsenal and other guns in the attic. It seemed to raise no red flags when he insisted on carrying a loaded gun around the house or greeted her at the door with a gun.

I knew a psychologist had evaluated Joe after his parents' deaths and just assumed that the sisters had been advised of the diagnosis. That diagnosis was that their brother was developing a serious mental illness. But no, they told me, they hadn't heard of the diagnosis. I was astonished at this revelation. I excused myself and dashed to my car to retrieve that earlier report from my briefcase.

Kelly and Kim grabbed the report from my hand, read it together and gasped to learn Joe's paranoia had been detected so long ago. It would have been such a simple, decent thing for the defense or prosecuting attorney to have taken the sisters aside and advised them that it was urgent that a psychiatrist see their young brother. Just the right word might well have averted another tragedy.

Joe proved to be the most frustrating client attorney John Nimmo ever had. The prosecutor had offered a plea agreement. Joe wouldn't go to trial and instead of the death penalty, he'd get a life sentence in prison without parole. Joe said no. Then, obsessed that he was blurting out secrets of his sex life in his sleep, he said he'd accept the plea agreement if his attorney would find him a doctor who would cut his vocal cords. (When I heard about this, I couldn't imagine how local psychiatrists concluded that Joe was competent to assist in his own defense.)

Well, Joe changed his mind about the operation.

"He's wired differently from the rest of us," an exasperated Nimmo kept telling me.

Mental illness, I said.

"He's evil," Nimmo would add.

Nonsense, Joe is mentally ill, I kept telling him.

The hearing for Joe's sentence was just about two years after he had sprayed sister Kelly's living room with bullets from an assault rifle.

I sat toward the back of the courtroom with Kathy Bayes, president of the local chapter of the National Alliance for the Mentally Ill (NAMI). Kathy had written a powerful column for the paper opposing the death penalty. Indeed, most letters to the editor about the case opposed the death penalty. Bishop John D'Arcy, a vocal opponent of the death penalty, added his words in a newspaper column appealing to the judge to spare Joe's life. We weren't the only people Judge Gull heard from. Kathy and I displayed newspaper editorials and articles about Joe at NAMI's annual convention in Chicago. Hundreds of people from around the country picked up the information with the idea of writing to the judge.

Judge Gull's answer was to announce at the hearing that she was not about to be influenced by public opinion. (As if public opinion had nothing to do with the death penalty being in the Indiana code.)

Prosecutor Bob Gevers, who earlier felt justice could be done by giving Joe a sentence of life without parole, turned in a theatrical performance at this hearing. His point was that this "cold-blooded," "remorseless" killer deserved to die. Gevers displayed four life-size photographs taken of the murder victims, showing the carnage in living color.

I felt the display dehumanized Joe's victims. The prosecutor said nothing of these young men's dreams, their hobbies, their love for friends and family. They'd been reduced to mere courtroom exhibits.

None of what the prosecutor offered suggested Joe was not mentally ill or that he might well have been in the middle of a psychotic episode when he opened fire on the four young men.

Gevers invited surviving family members to take the stand. They berated Joe, who seemed, as usual, impassive and unmoved by the survivors' anguish. It was striking, though, that only one of the four family members who testified said he wanted the judge to uphold the jury's recommendation of the death penalty. One woman presented Joe with a large Bible and admonished him to pray for forgiveness.

Sadly, nobody had words to comfort the victims' families.

Nimmo compared Joe's actions with that of a husband who discovers his wife in bed with another man and, in the heat of passion, kills them both. Generally, the courts go easier on such a murderer. I thought the comparison fell flat. No such outrage had riled Joe.

Nimmo then called Dr. Phil Coons to the stand. He's an Indiana University professor of psychiatry with a national reputation as a forensic psychiatrist—at the time the only one so qualified in the state. I had put the attorney in touch with the doctor.

In his examination of Joe, Coons discovered that, just as I suspected, the young man's sleeping disorder was a delusion. (Cellmates denied that he yelled out in his sleep.) Together with family history and other evidence, the doctor concluded that Joe suffered from paranoid schizophrenia.

This diagnosis meant that Joe's world is one where he's constantly menaced by others. He's given to uncontrollable outbursts. (At 15, he got mad at a television program, took his rifle and shot out the TV tube.)

Moreover, Joe's high intelligence, Coons explained, made it likely he would be able to conceal his most bizarre thoughts and feelings from those around him.

After they saw this doctor's written report, the other experts came around to this most serious diagnosis. On cross-examination of Coons, Gevers ridiculed it all. And, just as I could have predicted, Judge Gull mainly saw that the experts disagreed. After hearing a couple of hours of testimony, she read her sentence.

I had expected the death penalty. I couldn't have imagined she would declare Joe had "no mental disease or defect to consider."

He was headed for death row. I was headed for the chancellor's office at Indiana University-Purdue University Fort Wayne, to share a proposal I had been kicking around in my head about a major unmet need in our community.

People in criminal justice, attorneys and judges alike were in desperate need of an education about mental illness. Maybe it was too late for Joe Corcoran. But I was sure he wouldn't be the last person who suffers from paranoid schizophrenia to stand before Judge Gull.

Chapter Thirty-Four

THE NEXT JOE

Let's take a pop quiz.

Do people with mental illness always act crazy? Can they hold an important job? Is a person with schizophrenia dangerous? Is such a person able to express remorse for committing a terrible crime? Do anti-psychotic medications always work? Is a person who is mentally ill and found guilty of murder a threat to other inmates in prison?

Answering such questions can become literally a life-and-death matter for a judge such as Fran Gull and a defendant like Joe Corcoran.

Joe's case proved a sorry reminder that most of us couldn't answer such questions and, in fact, don't have a clue when it comes to understanding mental illness. I'd like to believe that can change.

After Joe's sentencing, I refused to drop the subject. I believed the community needed to make big changes in response to this terrible crime and what I regarded as a miscarriage of justice. It was with that in mind that I went to visit the Indiana University-Purdue University Fort Wayne chancellor.

Mike Wartell can come across as your standard, off-the-rack university administrator. Bearded, fluent, decisive, sure of himself, at ease before large audiences or in small meetings, he's both scholar and politician.

But in one way, he breaks the mold. I know of no college administrator who has been more passionate to develop programs that benefit the larger community.

I'd often heard him discuss ways the university, with more than 10,000 commuter students, could make its presence known in Fort Wayne. I was pretty sure he shared my opposition to the death penalty, as well as other progressive values.

What I proposed that muggy summer day was for the university to create a center that would draw on the expertise of people both in and outside the university to instruct folks in serious mental illness. I backed the proposal up with editorials. My immediate concern was to train the legal community.

Beyond that, I knew many professionals other than judges and defense attorneys regularly came into contact with persons with a mental illness.

I had in mind educators and managers in our stores, factories and other institutions.

My wife Toni, for example, was the principal of the county's largest elementary school. Every week in that job, she'd bring home stories of kids with major mental health issues, problems that interfered with their schooling and that of their fellow students. Yet few educators have been trained to identify mental illness, much less to deal with kids afflicted with such a disability.

Chancellor Wartell took up my proposal. A few weeks later, I found myself in meetings with professors and administrators from the university. But on the first go-around, the proposal for a center didn't move beyond the drawing board. Months passed.

Then, at the Jewish temple for a memorial service in honor of one of the university's professors, and an old friend of mine, I bumped into the chancellor. He promised to move ahead to create a center for the study of mental illness, for sure. Next thing I knew, I joined Wartell and other staff members at a local Vietnamese restaurant, the Saigon. Everyone in the group was enthusiastic.

He tapped Kathleen O'Connell, associate dean of the School of Health Sciences at IPFW, to head this new program. I was delighted. Earlier, I had enlisted her to be a member of the Suicide Prevention Council created to educate the community about the risk of suicide and respected her a great deal. Later, when the profs and I got around to mapping the center's work, we decided to include the range of mental health issues. We christened the new center the IPFW Behavioral Health and Family Studies Institute.

As it's been designed, the institute will offer short-term classes in mental health, provide staffing for the Suicide Prevention Council and address other mental health issues in our community.

Further, the institute will conduct research on the community programs that serve the mentally ill and others with mental disorders. We need to know what works and what doesn't.

Today, every time I hear of new funding for the institute, or how it has promoted other community programs or how many people have been trained in mental illness, I marvel that something good has come of Joe Corcoran's death penalty case.

Who knows what future tragedies the work of the new IPFW institute will prevent? How sad that will come too late for Joe Corcoran and his victims.

Joe Corcoran, whom I said was too sick to die

Chapter Thirty-Five

SAINT JANE

Once in a blue moon, in the save-the-world racket, you meet somebody so all-around good, it's a religious experience just knowing them.

For me, Jane Novak is that somebody.

There's a photograph that hangs prominently in my study. Jane stands among a dozen of us clustered around our square-jawed, smiling Gov. Frank O'Bannon. We have gathered to witness him sign a bill that requires employers to provide health insurance for mental illness that's comparable to the insurance for physical illnesses.

I'd judge Jane to be the shortest member of this group. In moral stature, she towered over us all.

Over my last years writing for the paper, the late 1990s, I saw a number of my crusades on behalf of the mentally ill win out. Parity of health insurance was one that merited big headlines.

I wrote the editorials. But the others in that picture with the governor also played a part in getting this victory for simple justice through the General Assembly. There was Steve McCaffrey of the state mental health association and Rep. Susan Crosby, the bill's co-author in the House.

Every time I glance at the photograph, my eye is drawn to Jane Novak, longtime volunteer director of the Fort Wayne affiliate of the National Alliance for the Mentally Ill.

I kept in touch with Steve, Susan and the other author in the House, Rep. Gloria Goeglein of Fort Wayne. But I worked most closely with Jane. For several weeks during the legislative session, I bet we talked on the phone almost every day. She was my best source, my cheerleader. I was her unabashed idolater.

Jane Novak illustrates a truth about social justice: Success usually comes down to the passion of a few people. If you wanted to learn how to be an activist, one who makes a difference, follow her around for a week or two.

Parity on mental health should be such an easy sell. You would think. It just means that companies would offer the same insurance coverage of an employee's depression that it offers for an employee's heart disease or cancer. Simple justice. But in conservative Indiana, no reform worthy of the name is ever simple. The Indiana Chamber of Commerce pounced on the parity bill. They were against it. I saw no evidence chamber bigwigs had investigated the facts. Chamber lobbyists conjured a dire scenario in which sharply rising health insurance costs would force employers to eliminate all mental health benefits or trim benefits for physical illnesses.

The warnings found their way into the editorials of the Indianapolis Star. That paper's conservative bent better suited that of the legislature than the liberal tilt of my own paper. So critics of the parity bill could wave a Star editorial in the face of advocates, which was supposed to have clinched the argument.

Back in Fort Wayne, Jane and I found ourselves trying to counter all manner of arguments.

In my editorials I laid out what the studies on parity laws in other states had found, how the extra costs of health insurance for companies were insignificant, measured in fractions.

The National Institute of Mental Health had spent three years looking at the few states that had parity. That study found an average premium increase of less than one percent. Another study even noted that premium costs actually dropped.

I went on to point out in editorials that decent coverage made it likely the person would seek help earlier, rather than later, when the illness had become disabling. For the employer, I argued, this meant fewer lost days due to illness and greater productivity.

For her part, Jane distributed my editorials widely throughout the state. Those went to legislators and policy makers. She also sent the pieces to family members whose company's insurance had been cut off. It seemed coverage didn't pay for more than a few days in the hospital when a loved one had developed a mental illness.

I advised Jane to tell her friends throughout the state to pick out just one argument or one piece of research from my editorials and stick to that point when they contacted their legislator. I knew that advocates, myself included, often overwhelm a lawmaker with so much information they turn off the person, rather than persuade.

I didn't need to tutor Jane in advocacy. I often thought that if it hadn't been for her, lining up supporters through a statewide phone tree, working so closely with other agencies, the bill wouldn't have passed. We would have had no group picture with Gov. O'Bannon.

I got to know Jane when our teenage son developed a serious mental illness. My wife Toni and I were desperate for guidance. Years before, out of curiosity more than anything else, I had visited local NAMI meetings. But when the issue struck our family, and we couldn't ignore it, I sought NAMI out fast.

I probably knew more about mental illness than most parents. I had always been fascinated by abnormal psychology, dating back to my undergraduate years. I had my own bout with depression toward the end of my teaching career, and was hospitalized in late 1972. (This is learning about mental illness the hard way.)

Yet it was Jane Novak who inspired me to get involved. She had come to the crossroad herself when her son Chip became mentally ill. He was still in college. She could either closet herself away from the world and place her son in an institution or she could do something about the plight of the mentally ill and their families. She chose to make a difference.

After a few NAMI meetings, she began to reach out to other families in crisis. At weekly meetings, I've seen her counsel a mother near despair over a son who had become psychotic. I've overheard her kind words to a husband at wit's end as he tried to keep his marriage intact while his wife rode the emotional roller-coaster of her bipolar disorder.

A retired caseworker for Social Security, Jane would advise families on how to get Medicaid for their loved one to help pay for the costly anti-psychotic drugs. She would listen to their stories with compassion. She'd reassure them that the family members weren't to blame but that their loved one's brain chemistry had gone out of whack.

Her message to them always was the same—blame genes, blame leaded gas fumes in the air, blame a virus, but don't blame people and, by all means, don't blame yourself.

My wife Toni recalls the first time she met this extraordinary woman. Knowing of our frustration with our son, Jane passed her a note saying that she was to call her any time, day or night. (It's no wonder that when she answers the phone, she often excuses herself, saying she's got a mother or father in crisis on the other line.)

She's brought nationally prominent figures to the city to promote fair treatment of the mentally ill. Among them was former First Lady Rosalynn Carter. Meantime, the national and state honors poured in for Jane.

But her greatest challenge has been combating the stigma of mental illness. The stigma is so pervasive. It defines and often destroys victims of mental illness, preventing them from seeking help out of fear they will lose face or their job.

It imposes upon the sufferer a sense of blame and a loss of self-worth. It leads employers to refuse to hire a person who admits to a history of mental illness. Families often shun the person. So for these people regarded as second-class citizens, the health insurance had been second-class, too.

In her lobbying, Jane did a lot more than persuade lawmakers in the fight for parity. She educated them about mental illness. She told them the saddest of stories, about families that saw their savings wiped out because insurance for mental health was so pitifully inadequate. Then, she'd let it all sink in—without pleading for the legislator to support her precious bill.

I've watched her work. First, you look at this retiree, a long-time member of AARP, petite, grey-haired, smartly dressed, with a confident yet humble bearing, and you think she's just a mom with a mentally ill son and a heart for those who suffer. Lawmakers would just tell her how sorry they were, then vote as they please.

Then pay attention to how she operates. You would see one of the most adroit advocates ever to darken the statehouse door to enlist some of the most bullheaded people Hoosiers ever sent to the legislature. The lawmaker who blew off Saint Jane could expect to pay for it at the polls.

During the debate over parity, week after week, she kept at it. She told more stories before the committees, the hardship of trying to pay the $8,000 to $10,000 a year for some medications. She button-holed the lawmakers in capitol hallways, and reminded them that recovery for severe depression is much more successful than recovery from a disabling heart ailment.

Her unfailing courtesy embarrassed her opponents. I recall once she uncharacteristically lost her cool debating Sen. Richard Worman from our area, a committee chairman. She not only apologized. She invited him to meet family members of the mentally ill and extended him such a gracious welcome it made him blush.

By signing the mental health parity law, Gov. O'Bannon made Indiana one of the first states to adopt this health insurance reform. Of course, the indefatigable Jane pressed on.

She urged the NAMI office in Washington, D.C., to bring Rep. Crosby and co-sponsor, Rep. Goeglein, to a national conference where they could tell people from other states about the victory. The following year, also at Jane's instigation I was sure, the national NAMI staff invited me to join a panel and share my role in the Indiana story.

Now I look with pride at that photograph of the bunch of us gathered around the governor with his right hand poised to put his name on the mental health parity bill. Most of us are smiling. Everyone looks proud. Jane stands in the back row, not taking center stage as might well be her right. Saint Jane requires no glory. In this moment of triumph, it is enough for her just to be there.

My sainted Jane Novak introduces former First Lady Rosalynn Carter

Chapter Thirty-Six

NICE COPS

As a rule, I limit my ride-alongs with police to "NYPD Blue" on TV. But for this piece of reporting, I made an exception.

It was the middle of the night in the tough central district of Memphis when I asked police officer Tony Mullins why he wore leather gloves with the fingers cut off. He said that sometimes chasing a bad guy he had to jump over fences.

That accounted for the gloves. He also led me to understand that he cut off the fingers so he could more readily flip off the safety and fire his Glock pistol at somebody about to shoot him.

Head shaved, burly, with an intimidating countenance, Tony isn't somebody you'd care to be on the wrong side of an argument with. All man's man, a cop's cop—that's Tony. But he has a finely honed skill you don't normally associate with a tough-as-nails police officer.

He is one of 150 Memphis officers on a team trained to handle a person with a mental illness in crisis. To observe Tony exercise this skill is what had me riding along with him that spring night.

Earlier at an evening banquet, he had been one of a half dozen officers honored as one of the top members of the Memphis Crisis Intervention Team.

I had gone to that city, along with Capt. Dottie Davis, who directed our Police Academy, and two other Fort Wayne police officers. We wanted to learn more about that city's CIT and to enlist the help of the CIT's top guy, Maj. Sam Cochran, to bring the Memphis program to Fort Wayne.

Memphis launched the CIT after a police officer shot and killed a mentally ill man, a tragedy that aroused the community, especially advocates of those with a serious mental illness.

Memphis wasn't alone. Most cities have experienced something very much like that.

It was 1992 in Fort Wayne when a police officer shot to death Leroy Ross-Church. He had been diagnosed as a person with schizophrenia. Not on medications, his behavior had become bizarre and menacing.

Holed up in an inner-city house, he threatened to kill himself with a knife. When police officers arrived, he locked himself in a closet. Then, as officers tried to coax him to surrender, he opened the closet door and lunged at them with the knife. One officer fired, apparently in self-defense.

These officers had received some training in mental illness. But nothing prepared them for how to de-escalate such a crisis. Ross-Church's killing might well have been averted.

I heard about the Memphis model at a national conference on mental illness. I found out that Albuquerque, New Mexico, and Portland, Oregon, had adopted that program. It made sense that research showed CIT training had reduced injuries to officers, as well as to persons in a mental health crisis. As an added bonus, because officers had become so skillful at de-escalating a crisis, the training cut the need to hospitalize people so often.

I was excited about bringing the CIT program to Fort Wayne. I went to Mayor Paul Helmke and spent an hour explaining how the program worked and its benefits. The next thing I knew, he had created a committee to study the Memphis model and to make recommendations to him and the police department.

I expected resistance. If Fort Wayne adopted the Memphis model, it would require big changes in how police handled the mentally ill in crisis and big changes in their training.

We already had a system in place. That involved two social agencies, a lot of personnel, routines the police knew and felt comfortable with and relationships built up over a generation.

For many years, police had been calling Ruth Anne Sprunger when they were on the scene where, say, a mentally ill person was threatening to commit suicide or was running in the middle of a busy street screaming at motorists.

The director of the Mental Health Association, Ruth Anne was regarded as the Florence Nightingale of mental health in the city. Whether it was day or night, she would get the officer's report, contact hospitals to make sure a bed was available and give a judge and a psychiatrist the details for their OK.

Meantime, the officer would transport the person in crisis to the hospital, stay with the person and await the official go-ahead for an involuntarily 72-hour commitment. This routine happened hundreds of times each year. Police understood their role because Ruth Anne had trained them.

Then along came Park Center. That's the community mental health center. And it gave her some competition. It created a mobile crisis team. This group took a share of police calls and joined the officer at the scene. The team's social workers and nurses would then attempt to de-escalate the crisis, maybe spending hours to get the person calmed down. No surprise. The Park Center team didn't always conclude that the patient needed to be in the hospital.

I saw this as a big plus over the way Ruth Anne handled the mental health crisis calls. For one thing, the face-to-face conversation between mental health professionals and the patient meant that the assessment of the person's need to be in the hospital likely would be more accurate than if that was done over the phone.

In turn, keeping someone out of the hospital carried its own benefits. It saved families the cost of the hospital stay. Further, research I was doing at the time found that hospitalizing a mentally ill person often had a poor outcome.

Of course, a person who truly represented a danger to himself or others—the legal standard for an involuntary commitment—needed to be in a safe place until they could manage things by themselves.

Yet even for Park Center to operate its crisis team, while an improvement over the old system, it still was costly, leaving the police without any meaningful role other than running a taxi service for the social agencies.

Moreover, whether it was Ruth Anne or Park Center's crisis team responding, if the person was involuntarily hospitalized, it would be for the 72-hour commitment. Until the Memphis model came along, nobody invoked the 24-hour commitment, state law allowed that shorter period.

Mayor Helmke's committee, while spending months talking, failed to act on the Memphis model. Understandably, Ruth Anne opposed a change. So did several judges. As best as I could figure out, Ruth Anne and these judges didn't believe a police officer should be making the call on when to take the person to the hospital. I felt that was a reasonable concern. Unless officers were better trained. And right there was the key to the success of the Memphis model.

Throughout this period of debate, I wrote editorials that I hoped would allay everyone's fears of this reform. And amid all the debate, a woman barricaded herself in her apartment, threatening to kill herself. For some reason, which I couldn't fathom, 16 patrol cars showed up, including the SWAT team with shotguns loaded with pellets—a sight that alarmed neighbors and escalated the crisis.

Finally, a plainclothes officer got the armed officers to back off. He talked the woman into surrendering peacefully. My editorial on that case noted that it demonstrated the need for a CIT program.

Months passed, however, and Mayor Helmke's committee failed to act on this reform of police training. Ruth Anne and a couple of others on the panel still had qualms about the reform. But a new mayor, Graham Richard, entered the picture.

Graham and I had been friends for 30 years. I had written the endorsement editorial that an attorney friend said gave him the narrow edge over his Republican opponent, Linda Buskirk. I doubted that. But it was fun to think of the paper being such a key player.

In one of Richard's visits to the newsroom, I shared with him a booklet on the Memphis CIT, prepared by that city's police department. When he came in for his candidate interview with the editorial board, he asked questions about the CIT that showed he not only supported the Memphis model but that he grasped its benefits.

Indeed, it wasn't long after his election that Capt. Davis, two other officers and I found ourselves in Memphis listening to Maj. Cochran and Dr. Randy Dupont, head of the psychiatric unit of the University of Tennessee Regional Medical Center, explain the Memphis program.

Mayor Richard and the new police chief, Rusty York, overrode the opposition to a CIT unit. A few months later, I had retired from the paper and sat with others in the community to interview police officer candidates. I was thrilled at the officers' desire to help and their caring for the mentally ill.

That first round of 40 hours of training produced 25 CIT officers. Today, more than 60 Fort Wayne officers wear the CIT pin. Ruth Anne has made her peace with the change. She still participates in training the officers.

Sgt. Tony Maze, who is in charge of the program, has inspiring stories to tell about our CIT officers. In the first couple of years the program was up and running, they responded to hundreds of calls. They've been able to talk people out of drastic action. They've nearly eliminated the need for the police to take any person with a mental illness crisis to jail.

Meanwhile, Fort Wayne has become a model that other cities in Indiana come to study. Dottie has made presentations around the state.

Throughout that night I rode with Officer Mullins in Memphis, it struck me that he may have understood more about mental illness than many psychiatrists. More than that, he had cultivated the patience to break through the wall of confusion to reach a person in crisis.

Like most CIT officers, he has gotten to know those persons with a chronic illness, checking in on them regularly, not treating them as stereotypes but as individuals deserving of respect.

That night in Memphis, we responded to one call that took us to a quiet street. Elderly women had called the police because a mentally ill man from the neighborhood had been pounding on their doors and walking up and down the street, talking to himself.

When we got to the scene, Mullins parked the squad car half a block from the man, then standing in a vacant lot, so as not to alarm him. The officer walked casually to the man and struck up a conversation, as if meeting him at the barber shop. Mullins returned to the squad car several times, visited with me and explained the man didn't want to go the hospital, although he clearly was confused.

Finally, Mullins informed me the man posed no threat to himself or others and, thus, we had no legal grounds on which to take him to the hospital for observation. He extracted a promise from the man not to knock on any more doors late at night. We drove off with the man waving goodbye.

We hear it all the time growing up: The policeman is your friend. In Fort Wayne, in just a short time, that's been a discovery for hundreds of persons with a mental illness and their families. If you've called a CIT officer to your home and that officer has defused a crisis, you can be sure that officer is your family's friend for life.

I doubt if there's a more respected, beloved bunch of cops in town.

Memphis police file

Officer Tony Mullins, who gave me a crash course in CIT

Chapter Thirty-Seven

REFUGE OF HOPE

My son John likes to say that the Carriage House saved his life. That's not much of a stretch.

Since it opened in 1998, he has had a welcoming place to go every day. He has real work to do. He has friends who could care less that he suffers from a mental illness. He has people who need his help. He has hope.

It's not always been like that.

I recall too well when he was released from one of his early stints at the hospital, in 1989. His psychiatrist had arranged for him to live at a group home for those with a mental illness.

He stayed all of a half hour. Residents appeared so bizarre, it spooked him. He called for a cab to take him home.

"What would you do if it were your son?" I asked the psychiatrist.

He had worked with John in the hospital for 10 weeks. He always gave me encouraging reports. At least that's what I wanted to believe. This time he was silent for what seemed like half an hour. Then he spoke.

"I'd cry."

Well, I did and more times than I care to count.

When mental illness strikes, it not only takes down the patient. It wounds family members.

I came to call them my heroes, the adult children, parents, the husbands and the wives in Fort Wayne who gathered each Tuesday evening at the mental health center to learn about this affliction that so isolates everyone who is touched and to support one another.

The illness creates zombies out of otherwise normal people. The depression, the anxiety or the voices in their heads immobilize them and destroy their incentive to join in the life of the family and the community. That's typical, even when the person's medication seems to help.

Imagine: No place to go, except to the doctor's or to group therapy. No job, no school. Too much pressure.

Day after day, they sleep or, awake, sit in front of a TV and smoke one cigarette after another. Even if they could work part-time, and be provided some degree of dignity, employers spurn them.

Until the Carriage House came along, that's been the story for too many people here with a mental illness. To appreciate what the Carriage House means for so many in our community, you have to try to imagine how devastating the illness can be, not only for the patient but for family members. I got into the habit of attending the Tuesday evening meetings.

Mostly, the families offered an understanding ear and a shoulder to cry on. Our little gathering made up one of hundreds of such support groups who are part of the National Alliance for the Mentally Ill—a quarter-million strong, or, NAMI.

I poured out my heart. I listened to the others as they told of the bizarre behavior of their son or daughter, husband or wife. I listened in horror as one woman told how her husband kept a loaded gun at bedside, how he often reported seeing strange people hiding behind the trees in their yard.

Once, a woman recounted how her son had told of getting messages through the television and armed himself with knives and how, in fear, she barricaded herself in her bedroom at night.

But more often, people talked of their frustration trying to get help for their loved one, getting frustrated with counselors and feeling discounted by busy psychiatrists. The ordeal promised no end, only occasional respites.

Underscoring it all, we spoke of this tragedy that had been visited upon someone who, before the illness struck, had been so full of life, of promise, of hope. So many times, I ached to reflect on how my son's illness had robbed him of so much.

"What a cute little rascal," the doctor in Bellevue, Kentucky, said as he completed a routine exam of this eight-month-old boy. Well, he was cute all right, and much more.

When John was five, a friend working on his doctorate in counseling administered an IQ test. The result, no surprise to his parents, showed a boy of a superior intellect.

His sister, Robyn, three years older and already with pen pals worldwide, seemed destined to be a foreign language teacher. The son, I reasonably fantasized, would go to Harvard and become an attorney in poverty law or a foreign correspondent. Years later, struck with a mental illness, John seemingly had no chance of realizing this potential. Then came the Carriage House, following the clubhouse model.

No, it wouldn't get John into Harvard. But it has given him something more important than a ticket to fame and fortune. It has given him a belief in himself and his worth. It has given him stature among his peers and a role certifying other clubhouses. It has given him hope.

I played a supporting role in the creation of the Carriage House. But it was Dr. Steve Glock, a retired orthopedic surgeon, and his wife Joyce who refused to give up hope when their son Chad developed schizophrenia. A popular and talented young man, he had been a state champion pole vaulter in high school and had every reason to fulfill the promise of his many talents.

For the Glocks, Chad's diagnosis shattered their dreams for the boy. Yet it didn't destroy their belief that something more than feeding him pills and offering counseling could be done for their son. In the mid-1990s, they investigated rehab centers for the mentally ill known as clubhouses. Why couldn't such a clubhouse be developed in Fort Wayne?

The granddaddy of all clubhouses is Fountain House, taking up a city block on West 47th Street in New York City. Back in the 1940s, a group of people with a mental illness decided to create their own refuge house where they'd have meaningful work and would treat each other with respect, as equals. Within a few decades, Fountain House had launched an international movement.

Clubhouses can be found in more than 200 cities throughout the United States and another 100 in 29 other countries, including Australia, Denmark and Japan. The club-house philosophy, codified in international standards, represents a break from the traditional treatment of the mentally ill.

In any good clubhouse, you're not a patient. You're a respected club member. You're not told what to do. You're not required to help in the kitchen, go to the meetings where work is divvied up or to accept an outside job in what's called "transitional employment."

The first time I visited Fountain House in New York, I fell into a conversation with a young woman who told how, as a nurse, she had worked for the World Health Organization in Kenya. I asked how long she had been on the Fountain House staff.

"Oh, I'm not on the staff. I'm a club member," she said. She truly was an equal.

As I was led from one unit to the next, I found most people busy, some preparing a meal, some working on computers, some posting new outside job openings and a few just visiting among themselves.

On another visit, I only learned after a much longer tour of Fountain House that the person who had just given me such an informed and detailed orientation suffered from a severe case of schizophrenia.

When staff members showed me the independent research on the success of clubhouses, I half expected what the results would be: The clubhouse does more to get a person with a mental illness back into the mainstream than any other program in the country. The clubhouse restores hope; yes, it saves lives.

Like the Glocks, I'd been sold from the beginning. They located the ideal property for a clubhouse. It was a large, century-old mansion, which had been used in recent years for doctors' offices.

Situated on five acres, along a busy street where city buses run, the building projects a warmth and charm that within a few years proved inviting to scores of persons suffering from a mental illness.

The Glocks put up the money to buy the property and enlisted other NAMI folks in raising more money for a renovation and expansion. I wrote editorials that explained the benefits of a clubhouse. Those raising the money used the editorials to give legitimacy to such a program when they went calling on the foundations.

Nobody showed more passion for the clubhouse than Kathy Bayes, whose husband, Guy, has suffered for years from a mental illness. Talk about dashed hopes, Guy graduated with honors from Duke, then completed a law degree at Yale, at the time the Clintons were there.

In the early days when NAMI members were raising money, John and Tom Shoaff came to see me at the paper. John is an architect; Tom had been the paper's attorney and had done legal work for me. At that time, they had their own mission. They were enlisting my help in opposing an expansion of a parking lot at the children's zoo, an effort they felt wasn't needed and which threatened the integrity of the larger park. (The Shoaff family had been involved in the city parks for generations.)

As we wrapped up our discussion of the zoo parking lot, I said that I also needed a favor. Could they help us raise some money for the clubhouse? (They already knew the paper would support their position on the zoo parking.) Tom Shoaff mentioned that a foundation board he sat on would meet the next day and decide on grants. He just needed a proposal, pronto.

When John and Tom left my office, I telephoned Kathy Bayes, the local NAMI president, at Lincoln National where she worked. She whipped out the grant proposal and had it in Tom's hands the next morning. Tom's foundation awarded the Carriage House $50,000, a godsend for the kitchen renovation.

By the time workmen finished the renovation of the old house, the Glocks, Kathy and others had raised more than $1 million. Meantime, they hired a talented veteran of the clubhouse movement, Warren Sparrow, to direct this new clubhouse, now dubbed the Carriage House.

I was able to get former Vice President Dan Quayle, who had served as the district congressman in the Fort Wayne area, to give the speech at the dedication. Dan's appearance was fitting. He was an original sponsor of the bill to establish "Mental Illness Awareness Week." The dream of the Glocks and many others was a reality.

In the first year, only a dozen people or so would trickle in for this daytime program. Within five years, the Carriage House would register more than 60 members on any given day.

My son John can expound the entire afternoon telling you what the Carriage House has meant to club members. I love the stories, too.

I think of somebody as shy as Burke—a student of mine 30 years before. He could gain dignity by developing a garden and speaking out in club member meetings. I think of Jason, who wouldn't speak to anyone at first. Then you find him standing before a crowd of family members to sing at the annual talent show.

The Carriage House helped a nurse who had lost her license gain the courage to return to school to win back that license and the right to earn a living again. People whose illness cut short their college have returned. Dozens, including my son John, have held part-time jobs.

As he explains it, sitting around and just talking about your problems doesn't build confidence. You just become more and more dependent. At the Carriage House, club members develop independence. They get a voice in the hiring of staff. Members select three of their own to sit on the Carriage House board, along with NAMI members and people from Park Center.

Because I now serve on the board myself, I'm a frequent visitor. It gives me so much pride when club members come up to me to tell me how much my son's friendship has meant to them.

"We love you," Guy Bayes, the Yale Law School graduate says as he wraps up a phone call to a club member who hasn't been coming.

You see this spirit of love manifested when tragedy strikes the Carriage House family. New Years Day 2000, just as word of good things spread at the clubhouse, Chad Glock, only 29, collapsed at Steve and Joyce's home and died at the hospital within an hour.

It was an undiagnosed heart problem that apparently had nothing to do with his mental illness or the medication he was taking. I doubt if the Glocks ever witnessed such an outpouring of love as they saw from Carriage House members. Much to their credit, the Glocks redoubled their commitment to this rehabilitation program that had held such promise for their son.

Director Sparrow would tell you that a person leaves his illness at the door. Most club members continue on anti-psychotic medications and most remain in therapy. But at the Carriage House, they focus on their strengths. It's a tremendous tonic. Members have an amazing range of talents. By unleashing those, people can be reborn. They can be seen by others as competent, caring and worthy of love.

Psychologist Carl F. Rogers called the kind of acceptance you see at the Carriage House "unconditional positive regard." How tempting to stigmatize those with a mental illness and to treat them as second class. But as Rogers contended, granting a person unconditional acceptance can transform a person—including, I might add, that person who has been among the most bruised, the most broken.

Today, when I see my son, I almost can't believe he's the same depressed and angry person I used to visit in the hospital and see struggle to keep his attention on our cribbage game. He's so outgoing now. A Bill Clinton-class schmoozer, he's known to others in the national clubhouse movement and belongs to a faculty of people who travel around the country to certify other clubhouses.

Is it more challenging to graduate from Harvard or to survive and even thrive with a mental illness? My guess would be the latter. For John and for hundreds more to come after him, the Carriage House has opened the door back to the real world.

Chapter Thirty-Eight

DOC

When I asked our county coroner, Dr. Phil O'Shaughnessy, to create a suicide prevention task force, the last thing on my mind was also enlisting a celebrity in the cause.

But a few years later I was standing in Mike Wallace's office and telling the legendary journalist why he needed to come to Fort Wayne to speak at a suicide prevention conference.

For real, there I was, in this cozy New York office overlooking the Hudson River, peeking at the photos of Wallace with famous people. And there he was, maybe the most feared interrogator of all journalists, telling me how depression had so weakened him and how it had fallen upon him like a black cloud during the trial in which Gen. William Westmoreland had sued him and CBS for libel.

Back when all this started, his own doctor had told him that he was a tough guy and should just buck up, not realizing that the depression had control of Mike's brain chemistry and that he was unable to fix it by sheer force of will.

By the time I met Mike Wallace in his office, I had been retired from the paper a year, my friend Phil had died of cancer and others had picked up the fallen mantle for suicide prevention in our community.

We got lucky. Kathleen O'Connell, associate dean of the School of Health Sciences at Indiana University-Purdue University Fort Wayne, agreed to chair the group. Right off the bat, she urged us to organize a conference at the university. My job was to make the contact with Wallace and persuade him to be our main speaker.

He was our first choice, ideal for such an assignment. But his secretary advised me that Wallace, a man now in his 80s, gave few speeches. (Nevertheless, Mike was still doing more "60 Minutes" segments than any of the reporters.) In fact, while he had appeared on "Larry King Live" to talk about his battle with depression, he'd never given a full-fledged speech on the subject.

His usual fee for a speech was about what you'd expect for such a celebrity—$50,000. But in e-mails, I asked whether, because of the nature of the conference, and his own personal brush with the issue, he would give us a break on the fee. Well, yes, he replied, he'd come for half the fee.

I'd like to think what won him over, agreeing to come in the first place, and for the reduced speaker's fee, was the story I told about Dr. Phil O'Shaughnessy.

When I met Phil, more than 30 years before, he headed the dental hygiene program at the university. I agreed to teach technical writing to the students. It was a required course then for one of those mysterious reasons that account for too much of college curricula. Later, when I was at the paper, and he had become the coroner, Phil would stop by my office during any visit to the newsroom.

Chatty, terribly bright, and in love with his work as coroner, he was a periodontist in the private sector. But Phil also trained as a dental forensics expert. He came to enjoy a national reputation, and he was often called in on major investigations. The detective work fascinated him, even the grisly work of identifying the victims of a plane crash.

But my guess is that it was the aftermath of the suicides that he had to investigate that most troubled him. Nobody in the community had tried to console so many families or done it with such sensitivity and caring.

When the county treasurer, depressed, desperate and confused, swallowed a cleaning solvent, Phil sat for hours with her husband and family at the hospital as the woman struggled for her life. That was Phil. Death's convener, he was life's champion.

I don't know whether I mentioned it to Mike Wallace but in one of my last conversations with Phil, he let it slip that he was still being treated for depression. The medication was Zoloft. That, coincidentally, was the same antidepressant that helped bring Mike Wallace out of the darkest days of his depression and his own thoughts of suicide.

Mike proved to be a great draw. No surprise. More than 700 people crowded into the ballroom and adjacent classrooms at the university's student union to hear him. He spoke movingly, without notes, for 40 minutes, then answered questions for another 20 minutes. The next day, before the workshops by suicide experts, Mike picked up where he'd left off the night before at a breakfast we held for local physicians.

I was nearly giddy over Mike's appearance and the rest of the conference. Naturally, I often thought of Phil. In his honor, his son Mark, a cardiologist, presented a plaque to one of the members of our group, Lois Hamilton, whose physician husband had taken his own life some years before. We were all becoming, in my mind, part of an ever-widening circle of people who understood more about suicide than we ever cared to know.

My unwelcome education came when I nearly lost my son. He was only 15, more than 20 years ago, trying to sort out his own life after his parents' divorce. He was troubled, depressed, to be sure. He had just completed a successful stay at a local psychiatric hospital. But back at home, he became extremely agitated, much out of character. Unknown to my wife and me, he had taken an entire bottle of an anti-depressant. They gave him the prescription for the medication when he was released from the hospital.

Alarmed, my wife called the police. They arrived quickly, but didn't see a problem. (This was before the creation of Fort Wayne's Crisis Intervention team.) They believed John's story that he had flushed the anti-depressant pills down the toilet. We weren't reassured the crisis had passed.

We insisted he be returned to the psychiatric hospital. We readmitted him and went home. We hardly had collapsed in bed when we got a call. John couldn't walk. His blood pressure had dropped. The staff had taken him to the emergency room at the big hospital nearby.

The hours we spent in the waiting room outside the intensive care unit rate among the worst of my life. When I hear family members who have survived a love one's suicide speak of their own guilt and shame, I know exactly what they're talking about. Years later, I saw my chance to change things.

That came with Surgeon General David Satcher's major report on suicide. He declared suicide an urgent public health issue, citing the 30,000 lives that suicide claims in the nation every year. But by focusing on prevention, other countries had dramatically reduced their suicide rates.

In this country, the U.S. Air Force, by training ranking officials in dealing with airmen and women under stress, cut its suicide rate by more than half.

I only needed to mention the idea of a task force for Phil to agree. A couple of days later, I got a letter from him that listed key players in mental health in the city that he had invited to join the panel.

I recommended a couple other names. I wrote an editorial that praised him for starting such a group. But at that point, you couldn't tell whether Phil's efforts would amount to much. For months it seemed the most the task force got done was to fashion two versions of a mission statement. Two of the psychiatrists originally on the task force dropped out because of busy schedules.

I recall showing up for one meeting at the City-County Building at the appointed hour. It was the fall of 2000, late November, and the country was still waiting for the results of the presidential election. By then, retired from the paper, I had joined the task force.

Phil was sitting alone in the still-darkened conference room, staring off into space. He wore a maroon turtleneck under his blazer. He looked tired. In a matter-of-fact tone, he told me his cancer had returned. He spoke of his disappointment but still sounded hopeful about the treatments.

Minutes passed. The scheduled time for the meeting slipped by. No other task force member appeared.

"Do you think people really don't care about suicide prevention?" I asked him.

"No," he shook his head. "They care."

Indeed, one by one they filed in. Soon the room was filled with apologies for the tardiness and with members of the suicide prevention task force.

We don't have any numbers yet to prove that the work of the Suicide Prevention Council has reduced the suicide rate here. (Dr. Bill Clark got us to change the name from task force to council.)

I assumed that bringing a national celebrity like Mike Wallace to town made the public take notice of the council. Police officers, social workers and others who attended the conference workshops no doubt know more about suicide than before.

Still, about 30 people in our county take their lives every year, a constant figure as predictable as the changing seasons. This translates into about 12 deaths for every 100,000 population, right at the national and state averages.

In one respect, this represents a tiny fraction of people in the community. But I often think about all the family members and friends who are traumatized by this tragedy. Even a suicide attempt can cause deep pain for everyone, as our family discovered.

Memories of a loved one's suicide don't recede in a year or two or three. So each year, in our community alone, another 30 families join a multitude of others still hurting.

To learn more about the impact of suicide, I invited a dozen family members—survivors they call themselves—to my home to tell their stories. Their group is known as "We the Living." Lois Hamilton, the physician's widow, is one of the founders. One couple told about their daughter who had made several attempts and finally succeeded. The husband of the county treasurer recounted the details of her death. To their great regret, none of these survivors understood the depth of their loved one's despair and sense of hopelessness.

I marveled that they had been able to carry on with their own lives.

I suppose most people have had friends or acquaintances who've taken their own lives. I haven't forgotten a one—the brilliant student I had when I taught in Cincinnati, the new principal who worked with my wife, the young boy down the street on Violet Court when I was a high school senior, the neighbor who hanged himself when I was a kid, the mayor of our town in Ohio accused of stealing from the city treasury, and, years later, a school classmate from bygone years who learned he had prostate cancer.

You can say it was a selfish act, they should have thought of their parents or husbands or wives or brothers or sisters. Nevertheless, from what I've learned, when you decide to take your own life, your thinking is so out of whack that you may well believe killing yourself is a gesture of love toward those closest to you.

But if we believe it's vital that we send rescue squads to retrieve a child who has fallen into a well or to dispatch firefighters into burning buildings in a hunt amid black smoke for survivors, should we spare any effort to rescue someone who has fallen into the hopeless pit of depression?

I know what Mike Wallace's answer would be.

I know what Phil O'Shaughnessy's would be, too. The Suicide Prevention Council, after all, is his legacy.

Courtesy The Journal Gazette

My old friend, coroner Phil O'Shaughnessy

Chapter Thirty-Nine

A GRANDFATHER'S WISH

If you have grandchildren, you're not surprised I dedicated my book to my granddaughters, Tanya and Cynthia.

They've enriched my life beyond measure. But I've got something to give to them in return.

This legacy is not merely an accounting of my crusades for justice, with a bit of personal stuff thrown in.

I hope my granddaughters, and others in their generation as well, will find a few things in these stories that inspire them to take up some worthy cause, perhaps even make it their life's work.

I can't claim that any one of my crusades is finished. None has been tied up in a neat package, the battlefields quiet, the victories forever secured. I only helped scatter the Philistines to regroup before they rise up again to defend the injustices of the status quo.

For example, it's tempting for a district to let schools re-segregate, especially after a court order no longer is formally in effect. And Fort Wayne Community Schools no longer is under a court order.

Besides, anyone who has followed the issue over the past generation knows that racially balancing a school is only half the battle of redressing the legacy of injustice that still bedevils the work of good people to make black kids successful.

Meantime, the suburban districts remain racially isolated.

Here in the city, the explosion of the Hispanic population presents a new racial balance challenge for school leaders.

Like the African-American kids, the Hispanic kids are being left behind. Both groups of kids are the ones you can guess will get most of the "F's." They're the kids whose reading lags behind that of the other kids. These are the kids getting more than their share of the discipline.

Meantime, Indiana, like most states, still transfers violent young offenders to the adult court and houses them in adult prisons. Yes, the kids are in separate units. I don't believe this goes far enough. What kind of counseling do they get? What kind of schooling?

I haven't found any evidence that the transfers do the kids any good or protect the public safety. Exceptions are rare.

Even if they've had a stint at a good juvenile center, the follow-up help to make sure they make it once they're released runs from the mediocre to lousy to non-existent.

Donna Ratliff seems to be a special case. A couple of years after she got out of prison, this girl who killed her mother and sister in a house fire looked like she was making it on the outside, with a job and a future. But she gets a lot of informal support from people who befriended her during the time she was locked up. That's not par for the course.

A few things I wrote about look like settled matters. At least the issue isn't in the news. I think restaurant owners have made their peace with the smoking ordinance. Even then, compliance hasn't been uniform and the ordinance isn't strictly enforced.

I'd like to think that the Crisis Intervention Team will always have a place in the Fort Wayne Police Department. It would only take a change in the city administration, however, to abolish it.

I believe the Carriage House is here to stay. But like all social agencies, it will continue to require generous financial help from the community.

On the broader question of the treatment of the mentally ill, our community has accomplished wonderful things. Yet it's only a start. A mere fraction of those who suffer from this terrible disability get the treatment that would let them participate fully in the life of the community. The discrimination against those who have a mental illness runs deep.

Finally, this I say to granddaughters Tanya and Cynthia. If you see people mistreated and dealt with unjustly, if you conclude a law needs to change or a new institution created, you won't be alone. I guarantee that a lot of people have noticed the same need, the same injustice.

Seek them out for they are your allies. Like you, they care.

They have talents. So give these people a call. Drop them a note. Together, you've got people as close as your next-door neighbors to heal, not to mention a world to save.

As my grandmother, Mom Hayes, used to say, "Don't just stand there, make yourself useful."

Family album

Tanya (left) and Cynthia, my granddaughters and muses for this book

Index

Books about Faith and Life
From LifeQuest

Hospitality: Life in a Time of Fear by Steve Clapp and Fred Bernhard. This book deals directly with the tough questions raised by the tragic events of September 11, 2001 and reveals that the answer to fear is not turning inward but turning outward. Learning to recognize the presence of God in others can have a liberating impact on all that we do and can enable us to move past the fears which threaten to immobilize us. This book shares specific strategies for practicing hospitality in our homes, our neighborhoods, our places of work, our automobiles, and our congregations. Clapp and Bernhard shares ways to deepen personal faith and improve our relationships with others. $15 each.

Faith Matters: Teenagers, Religion, and Sexuality by Steve Clapp, Kristen Leverton Helbert, and Angela Zizak. How do religious faith and congregational involvement influence the sexual values and behaviors of teenagers? This book reveals the results of a national study of 5,810 teenagers representing a broad range of religious traditions, ethnic backgrounds, economic levels, and geographic locations. The study shows that teens who are active in congregations are somewhat more restrained in sexual activity than those who are not involved in a faith-based institution, but these teens are far more sexually active than their clergy and parents expect them to be. The book offers strategies to help clergy, parents, and other concerned persons make a difference in the lives of teenagers. The results of the study were first released at a congressional briefing in Washington D.C. $16 each.

The E–Mail Diet Book by Martin Siegel and Steve Clapp. The typical employee in a business, university, or nonprofit setting receives an average of 85 e-mails a day. Increasing numbers of people feel truly overwhelmed by e-mail. *The E–Mail Diet Book* addresses questions like these:

- How can you deal with the growing volume of spam (unwanted e-mails) in your e-mail box?
- How can you keep e-mail from taking too much of your time and distracting you from other priorities?
- How can you maximize the potential of e-mail to improve your productivity and communication with others?
- How can e-mail be used as a force for positive change in the society in which we live?

Indiana University Professor Martin Siegel and prolific author Steve Clapp, friends since college, have teamed up to produce this practical collection of strategies which can transform how individuals and organizations use the e-mail medium. Having fun with the dieting analogy, they show how to gain control over e-mail and make the most of its potential. This may also be the only diet book on the market that contains chocolate recipes! $12 each.

LifeQuest
6404 S. Calhoun Street
Fort Wayne, Indiana 46807
1-800-774-3360
DadofTia@aol,com